9/08

The Terrifying Shark Attacks of 1916
CLOSE TO SHORE

MICHAEL CAPUZZO

CROWN PUBLISHERS ♛ NEW YORK

New York World,
July 2, 1916

Text copyright © 2003 by Michael Capuzzo
Illustrations copyright © 2003 by Lars Hokanson

For photo and newspaper credits, please see page 140.

Published by Crown Publishers, an imprint of Random House Children's Books, a division of Random House, Inc., New York. Adapted from the book *Close to Shore: A True Story of Terror in an Age of Innocence,* published by Broadway Books, 2001.

CROWN and colophon are trademarks of Random House, Inc.
www.randomhouse.com/teens

Library of Congress Cataloging-in-Publication Data
Capuzzo, Michael.
Close to shore : the terrifying shark attacks of 1916 / Michael Capuzzo. — 1st ed.
p.   cm.
Adaptation of: Close to shore. New York: Broadway Books, c2001.
SUMMARY: Details the first documented cases in American history of sharks attacking swimmers, which occurred along the Atlantic coast of New Jersey in 1916.
Includes bibliographical references (p. 138).
ISBN 0-375-82231-3 (trade) — ISBN 0-375-92231-8 (lib. bdg.)
1. Shark attacks—Juvenile literature. 2. Shark attacks—New Jersey—History—Juvenile literature.
[1. Shark attacks. 2. Sharks.] I. Title.
QL638.93 .C36 2003
597.3'1566—dc21   2002029918

Printed in the United States of America
April 2003
10   9   8   7   6   5   4   3   2   1
First Edition

CONTENTS

THE LAST MAN IN THE WATER

The smell of the sea pulled him east. The Atlantic spread before him like a pool of diamonds, liquefied. The young man couldn't wait to get in the water.

The sandy beach stretched for miles. Behind him were sea-grass-covered dunes, bleached fragments of shipwrecks, the shadows of Victorian turrets facing the sea. The warm wind carried the bark of a retriever, the faint perfume, so close, of the young women watching from the sands in their hourglass Gibson Girl dresses, their hair swept up high like the clouds captured in silk bow-tie ribbons. He was a handsome young man with slicked-back dark hair, a strong profile, a man who drew notice. He moved with the slight elbows-out jauntiness of a rebel, for ocean swimming was a new and godless pursuit.

As the young man paused to survey the beach, the dog came beside him and lapped his hand. The man put his toes in the water, then strode quickly into the shallows, the sandy muck sucking at his feet, for there could be no hesitation, no sign of timidity. As the water reached for his torso, he jackknifed his body and dove in. The lifesavers' rowboat, an old shore-whalers model, lay up on dry sand, beyond the seaweed line.

There were a few other swimmers, splashing and floundering near shore. Quickly he was beyond them. He was strong and practiced, with a lean, muscular body, and he moved swiftly into deeper water. He could hear splashing behind him, the dog playfully following. All eyes, he knew, were on him now.

Soon he had the water to himself, it was his ocean, he was without doubt the strongest swimmer of the hour, and he stopped, exhaled, and floated on his back, a signal to shore that he had done what he had set out to do. It is impossible to know what the young man was thinking as he floated. Perhaps he was thinking that he had come to a place of greatest ease, safety, and comfort. The whole summer stretched before him on the beach, with family and friends, not a care in the world but the European war "across the pond," which touched him not. Perhaps he was pining over his absent love, as a young man does under a summer sky with all of life ahead. The wedding was arranged. His whole future had been wonderfully arranged.

After a time, he realized he no longer heard the splashing of the dog. He turned over on his stomach and looked toward land: the beach was a distant, shimmering strip exhaling the day's radiant heat.

He was the last man in the water.

Postcard from Beach Haven,
New Jersey, circa 1915

LET US DO JUSTICE TO SHARKS

The big fish moved slowly on the surface of the deep. Its dark top matched the leaden sea; its white bottom blended with sunshine reflected from beneath. The fish moved with grace and beauty remarkable for its size, in a cloak of invisibility. Little about the scene had changed since the fish swam in the Age of Reptiles. The fish had appeared before the continents divided, before there were trees and flying insects, enduring while nature underwent upheaval and extinction. The fish had survived and changed little.

The Victorian scientific lust to classify and catalog every living plant, animal, and human tribe had made no inroads on the fish's privacy. Indeed, extreme scarcity is one of its greatest survival gifts. It was nature's plan for a minnow or a Maryland crab to be ordinary sights, but, like eagles in the sky and tigers on land, the great white shark sits atop the ocean's food pyramid, an apex predator. Great whites must consume such massive quantities of flesh to survive, it would be unthinkable for them to be numerous. It is, quite simply, too dangerous for there to be more than a limited number of their kind.

It was in 1916—and still is, almost a century later—a once-in-a-lifetime experience for a fisherman or a sailor to see such a fish. As a result of its great scarcity, little was known about the white shark in 1916. Most Americans had never seen a shark, except for scattered photographs in newspapers and drawings such as the comically nearsighted "*grand chien de la mer,*" vaguely resembling a great white shark, in Jules Verne's bestseller *Twenty Thousand Leagues Under the Sea*. The sailors' myth of a man-eating fish persisted in the machine age as a vaguely dubious relic of the Age of Sail. All the sea monsters of the ancients were shrinking in the glare of science: "It's scientific" would soon be the magic phrase that settled all arguments.

Myths of the sea had a way of enduring, however, even in the most rational men. It would fall to a new class of men, men who controlled and manipulated nature like none before, to expose the myth.

On a warm, windy afternoon in July 1891, the luxury yacht *Hildegard* steamed east in the Atlantic far from the dark New York skyline. Parties aboard the *Hildegard* routinely included such men as the captain's friend Charles Dana, publisher of the *New York Sun*; his newly hired architect, Stanford White; his fellow clubman at Delmonico's, Theodore Roosevelt. The captain was Hermann Oelrichs, international shipping mogul and one of America's richest men.

Oelrichs stood nearly six feet, more than two hundred pounds, a giant of a man for the time, with a great handlebar mustache and shining, arrogant eyes. An avid sportsman, Oelrichs helped introduce polo and lacrosse to the United States. He was also acclaimed as the best amateur baseball player and hammer thrower in New York City and the finest amateur boxer and swimmer in the country.

Yet that afternoon, as the *Hildegard* steamed east, Hermann Oelrichs made perhaps his greatest contribution. As his crew fed the leaping fires of the boiler, as servants distributed food and the men called out, "Gimme a smile" (a gentleman's term for a drink), and a raucous sporting mood swept over the passengers, there arrived a moment freighted with the need for spectacle. In that moment Hermann Oelrichs declared he was looking for sharks.

Oelrichs announced that so-called man-eating sharks were a fable of the ancients. Sharks were in fact cowardly, he insisted, and he would frighten away the largest of them that surfaced from the fathoms. That year Oelrichs had offered in the pages of the *New York Sun* a reward of five hundred dollars for "such proof as a court would accept that in temperate waters even one man, woman, or child, while alive, was ever attacked by a shark." Temperate waters he defined as the East Coast of the United States north of Cape Hatteras, North Carolina.

Now, aboard the *Hildegard,* a hundred miles from shore, several large sharks appeared starboard. Conversation ceased as the big fish moved silently, fins slicing high through the waves. Whispers traversed the deck as Oelrichs quickly changed into his bathing clothes. While side wagers were made, men snatched their white boaters against the wind, and women leaned over the railing to watch, long dresses whipping erratically. Others averted their eyes as the water received the powerful athlete.

Oelrichs disappeared for a moment, then surfaced between heaving four- and five-foot waves. Shaking the water from his brow, he stroked away from the boat, slicing through the waves atop a thousand feet of ocean. In ways unknown by the boating party, the sharks detected the presence of a large mammal thrashing noisily in the water and began to move in eerie concert.

Yet to the astonishment of the shipboard party, Oelrichs splashed boldly in the presence of the sharks, quickly scattering the most fearsome-looking fish in the sea. As the sharks disappeared into the deep, Hermann Oelrichs, flushed with pride and exertion, climbed back aboard his yacht, victorious. The passengers of the *Hildegard* cheered wildly, waving boaters, handkerchiefs, and scarves in the briny air. It is not known whether it was a harmless species or dangerous makos or

The New York Times, August 2, 1915

oceanic whitetips that had fled into the deep. A century later, scientists would not have been surprised to see any of these sharks avoiding a man. The big sharks attack in stealth or in defense, and a small, sluggish, finless mammal would hardly represent a threat. The truth of the encounter was impossible for men to discern that afternoon in 1891, and couldn't compete with the legend that reached New York City that evening: Hermann Oelrichs had conducted an experiment. The sportsman had swum among ferocious sharks, and sent them fleeing.

The great fish were no match for a man.

The moment would have been ephemeral, a parlor trick at sea, yet Oelrichs, like the fish he challenged, possessed his own qualities of myth. Fifteen years later, in November 1906, Oelrichs died at age fifty-six of a dissipated liver. He was eulogized on the front page of *The New York Times* as a major figure in the city's life for a quarter century, who might have contributed far more to society. Yet the mogul-sportsman went to his grave knowing he had won his wager. Indeed, his position on man-eating sharks had grown more convincing to the scientific community with each passing year. By 1906, the Wright Brothers had flown, the newly invented marvel of neon lights lit Broadway, Jack London had written *The Sea Wolf*. Yet scant more was known about the true nature of sharks. No one since 1891 had come forward with proof of a shark attack on man in temperate waters. Ichthyologists at the American Museum of Natural History in Manhattan, a world leader among the new and serious museums, were quoting Hermann Oelrichs's bet as compelling evidence that man-eating sharks did not exist.

By the summer of 1915, when Alexander Graham Bell in New York spoke to Watson in San Francisco in the first long-distance call and Ford made his one-millionth car, the editors of *The New York Times* adjudged it time, long overdue, for society to acknowledge the modern and scientific view of sharks. In an August 2 editorial, "Let Us Do Justice to Sharks," the *Times* noted that almost a decade had passed since Hermann Oelrichs's death, a quarter century since his famous wager, and no verifiable shark attacks on man on the East Coast had yet been reported. The editors were puzzled at the persistence among modern people of an irrational fear of sharks.

"To this day there is nothing that will so quickly set a crowd of swimmers scurrying for our beaches as the sight of a shark's fin in the offing," the *Times* lamented. Such fears were baseless and unreasonable, the newspaper's editors wrote. While the *Times* allowed that "the bitter hate that every sailor feels for the whole shark tribe can hardly be wholly baseless," the only evidence of such an attack was a single photograph, reportedly taken from a steamer in the Red Sea, "seeming to be a shark in the very act of closing his jaws on a man." Given Oelrichs's uncollected reward and the paucity of other evidence, the *Times* concluded "that sharks can properly be called dangerous, in this part of the world, is apparently untrue."

In the spring of 1916, the great white swam on the surface of a world that perhaps knew less about its nature than it had in several centuries. Even in the twenty-first century, the white shark remains largely a mystery. The force of its bite has never been measured. The bite of a six-foot lemon shark has been calculated at seven tons per square inch. The great white, at nearly twenty feet, three thousand pounds, will not submit to dental examination, and will not accept confinement. The fish is too big, too violent, beyond control. Man has never been able to keep the great white in captivity. When this has been attempted, the giant shark batters its head against its prison, unable to accept boundaries, hammering at the metal stays in the concrete that it senses electromagnetically. All that is known about the jaw power of the great white is that it must be immeasurably stronger than a small lemon shark's.

In 1971, Jacques Cousteau postulated that the white shark had poor vision. Now it is known that its eyesight is so remarkable that it can hunt, in rare cases, more than half a mile deep, its black eyes absorbing the faintest light. Until the late nineteenth century, scientists did not believe life existed at such a depth, concluding that the ocean floor was a lifeless plain. But when the transatlantic telegraph cable was hauled up for repairs, the thick cable swarmed with heretofore unknown creatures, a new universe. The first ocean scientists to explore the depths of that universe were alive in 1916, but their discoveries were decades away.

The fish's arrival was choreographed by nature to be mysterious. They could not have known what was coming.

male and female entwined. … hing rare in the ocean: the … carcharias, named from the … karcharias (shark), some- … 'the biter with the jagged … ared the womb with eight to … during gestation, the shark's … food = life. The life was very … iring the other pups. So the … cannibal. Twelve to fourteen … having won the most elemental … e born.

… four to five feet long, fifty to … ark had no air bladder for buoy- … moving, moving and killing and … ns and die. There was no playful … parents. The newborn shark fled … the nearest food source. Nature pumped her full of hormones that diminished her appetite temporar-ily. Mother's parting gift to her pup was to give it a brief window of escape before she devoured it.

The waters off Long Island were cool, to the shark's liking. Even to scientists in the twenty-first century, the birthing of *Carcharodon carcharias* is veiled in mystery. Yet the great white was probably born off Montauk, as early as 1908, one of the few places scientists have seen populations of pups.

In the Atlantic, off the eastern tip of Long Island, the fish moved at the speed of a walking man, so slowly it seemed hardly to be swimming at all. The slow speed was vastly deceptive. When aroused, the fish was alarmingly quick, capable of speeds of perhaps thirty miles per hour. It darted and fed gluttonously on small fish and squid in the early months. Its pyramidal head carried rows and backup rows of smallish teeth—baby teeth. Speed was its chief defense at this size, when the shark was young and vulnerable to larger predators. Like a mackerel or tuna, it flew on the power of a sickle-shaped tail, but unlike them, its skin was covered with thousands of tiny sharp denticles, miniature teeth that aided speed and stealth. The navy tried to emulate this design for its submarines but was unable to duplicate it. Speedo, the swimsuit manufacturer, succeeded in mimicking the denticles in its full-body suits to give swimmers added speed. But there were important differences. On the shark, the denticles were like razor-sharp sandpaper. A man who brushed against them would be instantly bloodied. The baby fish was a missile of teeth.

As winter approached, the waters south of Long Island gradually cooled. As a large predator, the great white needed a huge home range to find big prey, and cooler waters expanded its range. Soon the shark began to migrate south as far as the cooler waters and available prey would take it—in the winter, as far south as Florida. Come late spring and summer, the warm, wet season in the subtropics, the shark headed north.

Fortunately for everything else that swam, the great white grew slowly. Its body stiffened along three parallel muscles that ran from snout to tail. With the new bulk came a decline in speed, and the shark's narrow teeth, once ideal for snaring fish, broadened out so that catching small fish grew almost impossible. Adaptation was not difficult. The shark's

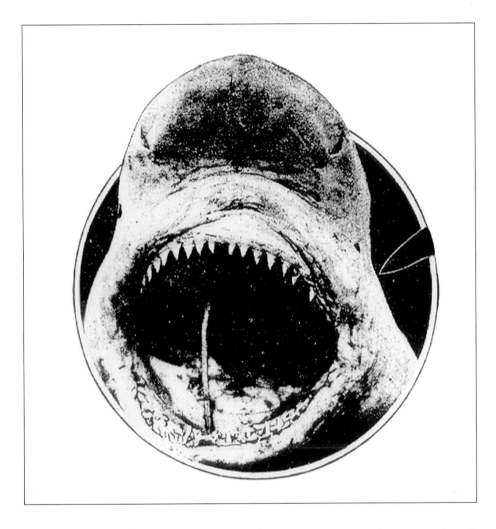

Philadelphia Public Ledger,
July 15, 1916

size and strength were enormous advantages now, and its speed still remarkable for its size. It was a lesson in survival, and the shark was survival's star pupil.

Like an infant child's, the shark's head had rapidly achieved adult size, expanding massively. Twenty-six teeth bristled along its top jaw, twenty-four along the bottom jaw. Behind these functional teeth, under the gum, lay successive rows of additional teeth, baby teeth that were softer but quickly grew and calcified. Every two weeks or so, the entire double row of fifty functional teeth simply rolled over the jaw and fell out, and another set of fifty rose in its place. White and new, strong and serrated. Broken or worn teeth were not an issue for the apex predator.

Little is known about the shark's appetite, except it was enormous, and like a man who didn't know where his next meal was coming from, the fish gorged itself. The waters of the subtropics, off southern Florida, had lured the shark that winter, emerald shallows crowded with prey. As the shark grew, its appetite shifted from small cold-blooded fish to large warm-blooded creatures, luscious with blubber and fat, rich with the oil that it would store in its liver for long periods to prevent starvation.

After eight years, the shark had nearly doubled in size—to almost eight feet and more than three hundred pounds—but was less than half grown. It was a shadow of the nearly twenty-foot goliath that would bite big sea turtles cleanly in two, shell and all; it was merely a juvenile. Yet already it was as close to invincible as a living thing can be.

Only two creatures in the sea, scientists believe, would be emboldened to attack a seven- or eight-foot great white aside from another, much larger great white. The first is speculative, but ichthyologists believe the huge sperm whale, armed with impressive teeth and already documented as an attacker of the giant megamouth shark, must also seize great whites from time to time. The second attacker of great whites does so rarely, it is believed, but an attack is documented. In October 1997, biologist Peter Pyle was riding his seventeen-foot shark research whaler near California's Farallon Islands when he witnessed "a very amazing sight . . . [an] orca with a ten-foot white shark in its mouth." Two female killer whales had been seen killing and eating a sea lion when apparently the white shark investigated and was not welcome. An hour later, the orca was seen pushing the shark along as it writhed in its mouth. But the orca did not consume the white. Instead the whale eventually dropped the eviscerated shark and it sank.

Yet the juvenile shark cruising in the subtropics knew no natural enemies and felt no fear. Perhaps it felt something resembling curiosity or excitement as it searched ceaselessly for appropriate prey, but not fear. The great white sliced through the cool, shallow waters of southeastern Florida with princely arrogance that winter. Amberjacks, dolphins, other sharks, and small whales fled its approach or died swiftly for their mistake.

nose

eye

ear

teeth

jaw

THE GREAT WHITE SHARK

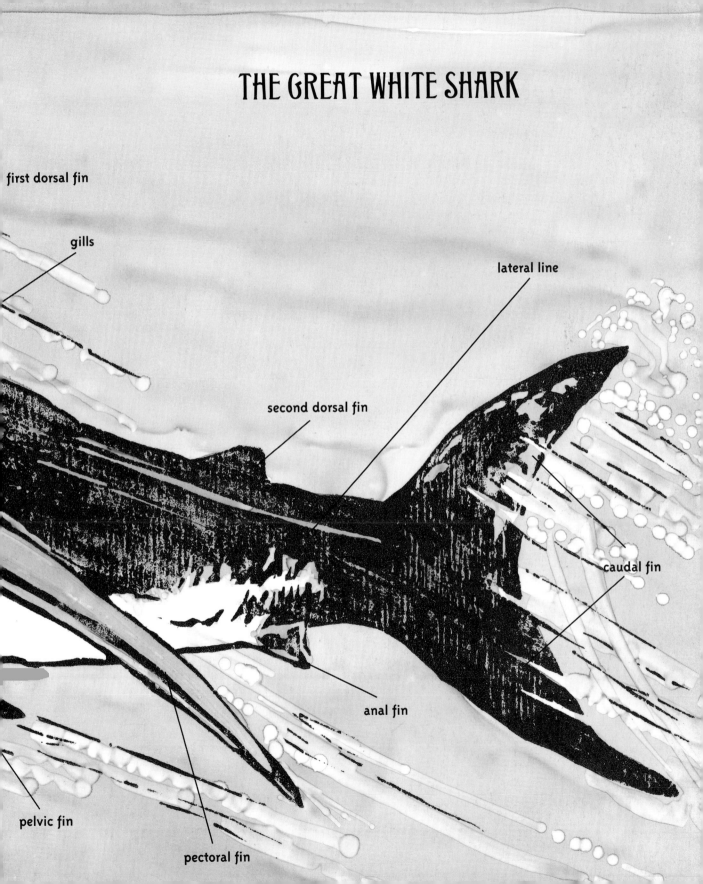

first dorsal fin

gills

lateral line

second dorsal fin

caudal fin

anal fin

pelvic fin

pectoral fin

All its movements were in shallow waters now, near shore. As a full-grown adult, huge and unassailable, the great white would be capable of open-ocean migrations, capable of crossing between continents in search of new hunting territory. Yet now it stayed near shore, near familiar and abundant prey. The young shark would range out in waters as deep as sixty to eighty feet and swim into waters four feet deep—or shallower, if it was chasing something. It chased seals up on the rocks. The young shark was equipped to follow its prey wherever it fled, almost all the way up onto shore.

In the late spring the shark was swimming slowly several miles off the coast of southeast Florida when it was seized by a current much warmer than its liking. The shark resisted, but the current was unimaginably powerful, a mighty river that swept the shark away from the shallow, familiar coast. The force of billions and billions of gallons of water tumbling with trillions upon trillions of tons of plankton and algae and uncountable fish—wahoos, tunas, dolphins, sailfish, blue marlins, and flying fishes—bore the shark away from shore. The current was miles wide and rich with prey, but the water was uncomfortably warm and deeper than it liked, and in this new environment the juvenile began to struggle. The young shark coursed through the rushing water, stalking yet somehow unable to kill or eat. The shark was not engineered to know fear, but perhaps for the first time in its life, it experienced prolonged failure, failure leading to hunger. The shark was still formidable and could sustain itself without food for days. It battled the current, but the current whipped along like moving walls, providing the shark with yet another alien experience—powerlessness. As it swam and tried to adjust to this new environment and grew hungry, the Gulf Stream, warm and wide and inescapable, carried the shark north.

A TRAIN TO THE COAST

By midmorning on July 1, the migration to the sea began. Across downtown Philadelphia, thousands of working-class men, women, and children, laden with rope-tied rugs and straw hampers stuffed with towels, bread, and sausage, bottled water and beer, made their way to the trams. Crowds thronged to Broad Street Station, where the Pennsylvania Railroad crossed the Delaware River to Atlantic City, Cape May, Asbury Park, Ocean Grove, Beach Haven. They were day-trippers who would return before nightfall, blistered and sunburned but proud to have participated in the new fashion of beachgoing. It was the largest migration to the shore in the city's history. The railroads of the Industrial Age had opened the seashore to the masses.

Twenty blocks west of downtown, the Vansants' servants hoisted great steamer trunks into two automobiles. The trunks were laden with silk and cotton clothing, damask linens, new wooden tennis racquets, swimming costumes, photographs and paintings, the portable Victrola. Both vehicles were filled to the rails with luggage—and with the Vansants themselves, Dr. Eugene Vansant, his wife, Louisa, and their four children, as well as their maids, cooks, nanny, and other servants. The Vansants traveled in the grand style of the last century and were looking forward to a long, soothing, and restorative stay in Beach Haven. The shore was a place to escape the congestion and disease of civilization. They were not especially comfortable with the invasion of the multitudes. Red-capped porters led the Vansants to a Pullman, while the hordes of passengers crowded the regular trains.

Louisa, reading the newspaper, worried about the potential ruckus awaiting at the Jersey Shore. Atlantic City—the glittering sea metropolis only ten miles south of tiny Beach Haven—was the seat of a rebellion. Under the headline "Startling Hosiery Fad Rules the Beach," the *Philadelphia Evening Bulletin* reported that ladies wore bathing socks rolled down instead of up, exposing the knee. "The mode is popular among the damsels who have dimples in their knees. . . . The lifeguards are primed to remonstrate if the craze continues. 'It draws too many sharks,' they explain."

The modern beach shocked Dr. and Mrs. Vansant. To the sea, young men and women vanished in roadsters. At the ocean they kissed in the seaside bathhouses. There was alcohol, dancing, suggestive songs. The dissolution of the formal nineteenth-century world they knew was first revealed at the beach, as if the restive ocean were the agent of change and the shoreline the advance guard.

The most shocking development was in the water, where the rising hems of swimming costumes became a battle line drawn by the Victorian establishment. In that summer of 1916 the cover-all Victorian skirt-and-trouser bathing costumes gave way to lithe, form-fitting swimsuits. The appearance of languorous female arms and calves in public roused a national scandal. On Coney Island, police matrons wrestled women in the new clinging wool "tube" suits out of the surf. In Chicago, police

A fashionable bathing costume, as shown in the *Philadelphia Press*, July 2, 1916

BATHING SHOULD BE INDULGED IN IF ONE GOES TO THE SHORE

escorted young women from the Lake Michigan beach because they had bared their arms and legs. The American Association of Park Superintendents stepped into the fray with official bathing suit regulations, requiring trunks "not shorter than four inches above the knee" and skirts no higher than "two inches above the bottom of the trunks." Police took to the beaches with tape measures and made mass arrests.

*Philadelphia Public Ledger,
July 7, 1916*

Dr. Vansant, reading his paper, was keenly interested in the War Department's recent analysis of the new class of German U-boats, said to be the most devastating marine weapon ever invented. They were capable of crossing the Atlantic entirely underwater, and according to the *Ledger,* mid-Atlantic seaports such as Baltimore, Atlantic City, Wilmington, and Cape May were the most likely targets of attack, for much of the nation's coal, iron, oil, and munitions was produced within an eighty-mile radius of Philadelphia.

An editorial in another newspaper that summer left the doctor pondering the new century. Noting an unusual occurrence of wars and revolutions, strange crimes, divorces, heat waves, and unforeseen hurricanes, the editorial writer pondered the possibility that technology had destroyed a natural equilibrium, setting something amiss in this "erratic era":

> Mariners tell of strange storms arising, seemingly, from convulsions beneath the deep rather than in the heavens above. Can it be that the forces of destruction let loose by man have been mighty enough to put the universe out of whack? Is it possible that our submarine prowlings and torpedoings have disturbed the Atlantic currents? Something certainly is wrong somewhere.

Trailing a pennant of thick black coal smoke, the Beach Haven Express steamed toward the glittering sky, the freshening breeze. Five miles from the coast, over the Manahawkin meadows, Charles Vansant and his sisters were forced to shut the windows as mosquitoes, gnats, and greenhead flies swarmed the car. The Pullman grew suffocatingly hot.

The Pennsylvania Railroad's Beach Haven station rose nobly from the quagmire overlooking awesome stretches of sea grass and swamp. A porter from the Engleside Hotel rushed forward to hoist suitcases and steamer trunks onto the island's first motorized vehicle. As Charles disembarked, he posed for a photograph, standing proudly next to the giant black Pennsylvania steam engine, his eyes bright with summertime joy. Seeing his son standing by the railroad engine pleased Dr. Vansant, for the boy was at last coming into his own. The young man who disembarked at Beach Haven was not just clever but capable, a son a father could be proud of.

The Engleside autobus

The porter signaled the official start of vacation as he cried, "Engle-siiiiide!" and ushered the final stragglers aboard the autobus. In a few blocks the autobus turned and there, facing the sea, was the massive Engleside Hotel. Bunting draped the long veranda on the front of the hotel, American flags flew from porches and peaked roofs, streamers rose from the portico to the turret five stories above.

Through the portico was a changeless world, an Edwardian parlor by the sea. Out on the veranda, gloved waiters served English tea and pastries and offered Philadelphia newspapers. The hotel was a temperance house, but guests enjoyed the pleasures of reading, dining, dancing in the starlit evening, rowing on the moonlit bay, writing long, intimate letters, and waiting for the return mail. Gentlemen and

The Engleside Hotel

ladies in promenade dress took stately constitutionals, enjoying the grandeur of the sea from the boardwalk, lifted safely above the muddle of sand and tide. Tennis players volleyed on the clay courts by the ocean, near the grand bathing pavilions, and as the light deepened just so, two or three men and women could often be seen practicing the new fad of plein air painting, recording azure and sapphire seas. On the beach were potato-in-spoon races, skits with parasols, violins,

Lobby of the
Engleside Hotel

and leaping dogs—entertainments that diverted the guests from rumors that the kaiser's U-boats were trolling offshore.

In his office under the great spire, hotelier Robert Fry Engle reviewed the bookings for the Independence Day weekend with great satisfaction. For the second consecutive year, all 150 rooms were sold out from July Fourth straight through Labor Day. Engle, like his late father, disapproved of the immoral and noisome behavior of some of

A dining room at the Engleside

Tennis players
at the Engleside

his more modern guests. But there was no denying the wonderful impact of the new horseless carriage and the railroads ferrying middle-class tourists en masse to the seashore, whatever their nouveau morality. The Engleside had never experienced such a boom.

As the day came to its end, Louisa Vansant, wearing a long dress and a wide-brimmed hat, lifted her train and led her daughters downstairs for the customary twilight stroll before dinner. Louisa found her son on the wide beach playing with a dog. At this hour the sea was nearly deserted and Charles, frolicking with the large, energetic retriever, had drawn attention. It swelled Louisa's heart to see what a fine young man he had become, but it was a bittersweet sight, too; it was Charles's last summer away with the family before he married and started his own family, his own life.

Louisa and the girls joined the doctor on the boardwalk. The Vansants stood looking out over the sea, enjoying the light breeze, the grandeur of the ocean, and the knowledge that a fine dinner and a comfortable bed awaited. The moment was crowned by the joyful sight of Charles charging into the surf and, to the delight of the small crowd of onlookers, the dog leaping after him into the waves. Splashing and kicking in tandem, trailing a wake of bubbles and froth, man and dog began to swim.

The Beach Haven boardwalk, circa 1912

THE SEA MONSTER

The great white shark's migration north along the Eastern Seaboard of the United States was normally a thoughtless, instinctual action, but the young great white faced pressing problems now. Competition among the large predators in the Gulf Stream was intense. But after days, the great current passed on without it. Somewhere approximately seventy miles east of New Jersey, a looping wave, a fluke current, whirled the shark out of the mighty stream. Suddenly the crowds were gone.

The young great white was lost, pulled by a stray plume of the Gulf Stream. Six hundred feet beneath the shark, a short dive for a great white, the continental shelf was lush in bottom fishes—rake and cod, ling and porgies—but this shark had grown used to hunting the surface and passed over the bottom feeders.

Perhaps it was attacked and injured by a larger predator. What motivated it is unknown. What is known is that it became a rare "rogue" member of its species—a deranged individual apex predator—a behavior seen in man-killing lions and elephants in Africa. And in human beings. "It was the equivalent," says ichthyologist George Burgess, "of a serial killer." At the dawn of the twentieth century, this comparison was not yet available, as human serial killers were not known. In the parlance of the time, the shark was a sea monster.

Soon other currents and scents, like the ones that had snatched it into the giant stream, began to work on the young shark, pulling it west. Prey was still scarce, its hunger growing, but the water was getting shallower and all its senses told it that this at least was a good thing. It was nearing shore and more abundant prey.

Most of the great white's brain is given over to enormous olfactory lobes, and thus it has been called a "brain of smell." It can smell prey a quarter mile away. Sharks have been observed, writes Thomas B. Allen in *The Shark Almanac,* trailing bathers in the shallows who had scratches on their legs. According to the zoologist A. D. Hasler, "We are concerned here with a sense of such refined acuity that it defies comparable attainment by the most sensitive instruments of modern chemical analysis."

Seven miles from shore, the shark began to smell the rich cocktail of organisms washed to the coastline from rivers and inlets swollen with heavy summer rain. This triggered an ingrained message: prey. But it smelled something else, something that didn't fit the automatic profile to hunt, something that the great white would experience as a mild curiosity . . . a strong, disconcerting lure. Human waste, the product of urban development, was being pumped off the New Jersey coast then for the first time.

Two to three miles from shore, the shark's progress was slowed by a vast net suspended perpendicular to the coast, stretching six miles straight out to sea and covering every inch of potential passage from the surface to the bottom of the ocean. This was the first of some twenty-five fish "pounds" strung along the coast of Long Beach Island. The pound was framed on three sides and the bottom with great nets, forming an immense boxed trap. The island's thriving pound industry, second only to tourism, landed ten million pounds of fish a year. Even if the traps were now empty, the coastal waters were habitually flush with the by-product of this industry— guts and other offal from cleaned fish—a cocktail of the living and the dead that drew the shark toward shore.

And something else, people of the time believed, attracted the shark.

Another "sea monster," black and torpedo-shaped and glistening with dark water, surfaced on the East Coast later that night. It was the German U-boat *Deutschland*, 315 feet long, the largest submarine ever built and the first to cross the Atlantic. It inspired awe and fear, and the press described it as having "eyes like a monster sea dog"—an ancient reference to the great white shark.

The *Deutschland* slipped beneath the English blockade and four thousand miles of waves. Although it was carrying only cargo, not weapons, as a German U-boat it alarmed Americans—the previous year a U-boat sank the passenger liner *Lusitania*, killing 128 Americans. For the rest of the summer of 1916, the great white shark and the German U-boat would be linked, in editorials, cartoons, and letters to the editor, as invading twins of darkness on an innocent American shore. People speculated that the submarine attracted the shark as they shared the same waters, but in fact if the shark had ever spied the U-boat—thirty-five times larger than itself—it would have simply fled.

But sensing intense organic activity, the young white picked up speed, perhaps to five miles an hour, in the direction of shore.

THE NIGHTMARE OF CENTURIES

Charles stood knee-deep in the shallow surf, feet planted on the soft golden sand, the outgoing tide gently swirling about his calves. Ahead bobbed the diving platform Robert Engle had installed in front of his hotel for the new season; in the distance floated a line of salmon clouds. Behind him he could hear the dog splashing. The dog was paddling hard now, approaching fast. Charles knew without looking—an instinct all mammals share—that something was bearing close, and he reacted instinctively and dove to stay ahead of the dog: two species playing, communing across the waves.

As man and dog swam out in a line, they joined the sweeping canvas the ocean offers the shore. Charles closed his eyes as his face turned rhythmically into the sharp, cold brine, feeling the rush of coolness along his torso as he stroked in measure with the cadence of the swells. The dog kicked with all four legs beneath the surface, a force that lifted its head above the waves and left its shaggy tail floating in a trail of froth.

Far out at sea, swimming steadily, the young shark received a faint signal. Currents were washing against the thin steel cable that rooted the diving platform of the Engleside Hotel to the bottom, causing it to vibrate and issue infinitesimal waves of sound. These waves exploded seven miles out to sea in less than eight seconds, moving at more than three thousand miles an hour, rhythmic, constant, reaching a sensitive line of nerves embedded in the head of the fish, the head that turned slowly side to side to improve the chances of favorable reception. The faint sound waves grew stronger, more regular, and the shark made a tiny adjustment in direction. The great fish swam directly into the wave of sound and began, ever so slightly, to move faster.

Emerging from the deep, in perhaps fifty feet of water, the shark sensed something different. Long, powerful, irregular noises began to batter its conical head, a wild mixed signal. An image appeared in its brain, an electronic projection, a pulsing outline of two objects moving near the surface. The shark could detect microscopic urine particles in the water: mammals. Each movement broadcast sounds and scent and an electronic trail, an aura of impulses.

Charles was the strongest swimmer in the water now, his arms and legs indicating one thing to the shark: large prey. Then there was the dog. It is now known that a man who swims in shark-infested waters with a dog greatly enhances his odds of being attacked. According to ichthyologist George Burgess, who directs the International Shark Attack File, "The irregular swimming actions of animals are extremely attractive to sharks." In 1987, off Panama City, Florida, a man jumped from his boat to go swimming. His girlfriend lowered his poodle into the water, and within moments a large bull shark removed much of the man's leg, killing him instantly. The Shark Attack File is filled with accounts of sharks drawn to human victims by the erratic thrashing of a paddling dog. That afternoon in 1916, sound waves from the seventy-five-pound dog drummed on the great fish's head with feral intensity, a jagged, broken signal of distress. Charles stroked smoothly and happily, unaware he was being profiled. The great white was closing in.

A small crowd on the beach watched as Vansant stroked out beyond the breakers. They were in that moment standing on the edge of time, wise in ways moderns are not, educated in the classics and myths, more in touch with the sea. But these people lived before modern oceanography, before radio and television, and were no more prepared to witness the first man-eating shark in American history rise from the waves than to see Captain Nemo's *Nautilus* surface from the abyss. Who could blame them if they saw a "sea monster"?

In the late afternoon of July the first, Charles was swimming the Atlantic to see how far he could go, and his desire to set himself apart led him to violate a fundamental rule of nature: Stay with the group. A lone mammal, exposed and vulnerable, invites a predator. In a study of great white shark behavior by George Burgess and Matthew Callahan using data from the International Shark Attack File, no other humans were within ten feet of the victim in 85 percent of the attacks.

Fifty feet away, the great white was mulling whether to attack. Far from our image of a mindless killer that overwhelms its victims, the great white takes no chances when challenging prey. But once a great white decides the odds favor it, the decision is beyond appeal, the attack relentless.

As the crowd on the beach studied the tableau of man and dog, suddenly, with no apparent reason, the retriever turned back toward shore. Witnesses thought the dog tired out, simply swam too far. Charles turned around, too, treading water, and called out to the dog, enticing it to return. But the retriever, climbing onto the beach, shook itself off and remained on the sand. On the boardwalk and beach, people waited for a resolution to the drama. The Vansant girls saw Charles give up the game. He was coming in.

But as Charles swam toward shore, a bystander on the beach noticed something odd. A dark fin appeared in the water behind the young man. At first it was mistaken for a porpoise, a sight people were accustomed to then. But porpoises were known to roll in schools parallel to the coast; this fin was alone and moving swiftly toward shore in the direction of the young man. Someone on the beach cried across the waves, "Watch out!" As the fin approached, the chorus grew: "Watch out! Watch out!"

But Charles could not hear the warnings. He was turning his head in and out of the water in a rhythmic crawl. The great white could see his prey now with startling clarity, making what followed even more unusual. For in the great majority of shark attacks on humans, sharks are hurtling through roiling, cloudy water in which they must strike quickly to seize their prey. The flash of a pale foot resembles the darting of a snapper, a belt buckle winks in the sun like a fish scale, and the shark bites. But the great white saw Charles Vansant clearly and kept coming. In the last instant it detected the final confirmation of *mammal:* the blood pounding through Charles's veins. The thumping of his heart.

In that moment, an awful feeling swept over Vansant as the continued cries, louder now, of "Watch out!" rang from the beach. Seconds before the attack, a shiver traveled down his spine—humans are gifted, as are all large mammals, with the instinctive ability to detect that they are being hunted. As the creature's shadow merged with his on the bright, sandy floor of the sea, Charles experienced an adrenal explosion, the overpowering natural urge to live. He was in only three and a half feet of water, close to shore. Safety was at hand. But it was too late.

The great jaws rose from the water, a white protective membrane rolled over the eyes, fifty triangular teeth closed, and man and fish splashed in a spreading pool of blood. One bite. One massive, incapacitating bite tearing into the left leg below the knee. Charles screamed—a scream that resonated to the beach and tennis courts and veranda. The attack had taken less than a second, but now time began to slow down. His parents and sisters and the crowd of onlookers stood transfixed in horror and disbelief. "The young man was bathing in only three and a half feet of water," remembered W. K. Barklie, a Philadelphia businessman on the beach that day. "We thought he was joking until we saw the blood redden the water."

Charles still screamed, numb with terror, trying to free himself from the vise of fifty large serrated teeth, but he, too, had little idea what was happening to him. Despite the gruesome wound, he felt a minimum of pain. As strange as it seems, it is common for shark attack victims to experience "painless torture"—to greatly underestimate the severity of their wounds.

Charles's struggle to free himself only tightened the shark's grip on his femoral artery: the great teeth ground down to the bone. Louise, Charles's sister, kept her wits about her as she witnessed a sight she would never forget: "Everyone was horrified to see my brother thrashing about in the water as if he were struggling with some monster under the surface," Louise recalled. Then, as if a spell were broken, men entered the water to rescue the young man.

What followed baffled shark researchers for decades: The great white backed off in the red-tinged surf, pieces of Charles Vansant's calf and femoral artery in its mouth, and appeared to be waiting. Twenty years later, in Buzzards Bay, Massachusetts, a great white provided a clue to the shark's behavior. A fourteen-year-old boy swimming in shallow water was savagely bitten by a great white. As the boy screamed and floundered in a balloon of blood, the shark was observed "standing off in the blood-reddened water but a few yards away, seemingly ready to make another attack."

The reason is brutally simple, according to John E. McCosker, director of San Francisco's Steinhart Aquarium. The great white employs a classic predatory technique once practiced by the saber-toothed tiger.

The extinct tiger hunted the woolly mammoth by biting it once and standing back. Avoid needless confrontation. Expend no more energy than necessary. Take no chances.

The great white was waiting for Vansant to bleed to death.

First to reach the surf line was Alexander Ott. His decision to enter bloodied water took extraordinary courage, but by the time he reached Vansant in waist-deep water, the shark had vanished and the young man was struggling not to drown in a cloud of his own blood. Quickly, Ott hoisted Vansant under the arms and began to tow him to shore. It was then that Ott felt a powerful tug in the opposite direction, and realized with horror that the shark had hit Vansant again and fastened to his thigh. The shark and Ott were in a tug-of-war with Vansant's body. The shark appeared to Ott to be black, ten feet long, and five hundred pounds. It was unimaginably strong, he thought. He cried for help.

More men rushed into the water and formed a human chain with Ott, frantically trying to free Vansant from the jaws of the shark. Vansant was still conscious, struggling to escape, but the great teeth held fast. The human chain had succeeded in pulling Charles nearly to the beach—but the great white followed, its massive conical body scraping the sands. The monster was coming onto the beach. Then, suddenly, it was gone, a whirl of foam trailing the dark fin as it submerged.

Profound shock momentarily seized the people on the sands. They had no context for what had happened; there was no way for them to know that sharks, in other times and other lands, followed their human victims right up onto land. There was no way for them to know that the popular new sport of recreational swimming, fueled by expanding wealth, industry, and human population, had brought the nightmare of centuries of sailors to shore.

Charles lay crumpled on the beach, bleeding profusely. Men and women rushed to his side, some out of love, others out of morbid curiosity; still others, unable to look, turned away. Louise Vansant, who had kept her composure during the attack, almost fainted when she approached her brother. "The terrible story was revealed," she said. "His left leg had been nearly torn off."

Dr. Eugene Vansant flew down the boardwalk steps, onto the sand, and rushed to the fallen figure of his son. Ott and Barklie moved aside to make room, and Eugene kneeled on the beach and took Charles's hand. The young man was lying on his back, his left leg a bloodied mass, blood pouring from the wound and pooling with the soft, receding tide. His face was a ghastly white, and he moaned in pain, reeling toward unconsciousness. Eugene put his fingers to his son's wrist; the boy's pulse was weakening. His eyes signaled that he recognized his father. There was little time.

Dr. Vansant removed his jacket and vest, rolled up his sleeves, and ordered that no one touch the wound. Germ theory was one of the principal findings of Dr. Vansant's lifetime, and Vansant operated in sterile whites instead of a black business suit, as he had once done. But no modern supplies were available now. The doctor's mind raced. He had never seen such a wound. What in the Lord's name had caused it? Was it suffused with animal poisons? It looked like a wound of war, but it was a bite. Nothing could be done, Dr. Vansant realized, until the bleeding was stopped.

Alexander Ott tore strips of fabric from a woman's dress to use as a tourniquet, but the rush of blood barely slowed. Soon Dr. Herbert Willis joined Dr. Vansant at his son's side, along with Dr. Joseph Neff. The three medical men inspected the wound and conferred. A fish bite of such magnitude was outside their experience. Robert Engle suggested they move the young man back to the hotel, where there was water, soap, and bandages. Dr. Vansant helped carry his son to the hotelier's office. There the men quickly unscrewed the hinges of Engle's office door and laid it across two desks as an operating table.

Dr. Vansant assisted in cleaning and bandaging the wound, but the bleeding remained profuse, and it was soon evident that in the hour of his son's direst need, Dr. Vansant wasn't quite sure what to do. The wound was so severe that the doctors feared Charles wouldn't survive an automobile ride to the nearest hospital in Toms River, thirty miles northwest. Half a century later, Vansant's wound would have been considered relatively minor for a shark attack, medium-severity arterial damage, which "the victim usually survives if correct [modern] treatment is administered on the beach," according to South African doctors D. H. Davies and G. D. Campbell in *The Aetiology, Clinical Pathology and Treatment of Shark Attack*. But that evening, at six-forty-five, an hour after he entered the water for a swim, Charles Vansant died of shock and massive hemorrhaging on Robert Engle's office door. Dr. Vansant looked on helplessly as his son died.

That evening a hush fell over the Engleside dining room. But after dinner, hotel guests cornered fishermen and baymen and other wizened veterans of the shore who drifted on and off of the veranda all night long. The number of people who had witnessed the attack seemed to grow by the hour. Robert Engle tried to remain stoic and calm as reporters from Philadelphia newspapers scuttled about the lobby and veranda, questioning his guests. Disagreements and arguments broke out, until finally a consensus emerged of suspects in young Vansant's death: a giant tuna, a shark, but most likely a great sea turtle, which had the power, the fishermen said, to snap a man in half.

The attending physician had a different opinion. He recorded the primary cause of death on Vansant's death certificate as "hemorrhage from femoral artery, left side," with the contributory cause being "bitten by a shark while bathing." It was the first time a shark bite had appeared as an official cause of death in U.S. history. Seeking to reassure his guests, Engle stood and declared bathers had nothing to worry about—the next morning, the hotel would erect a netting around the beach strong enough to block German U-boats. Swimming in the clear, paradisal waters of the Engleside would go on as usual.

But a somber mood pervaded the Engleside that evening as one by one the hundreds of room lights winked out. A new and nameless fear had seized the guests, a fear of the unknown as well as a fear of the sea. Even those who watched the attack had little notion of what they had witnessed, except to agree, as W. K. Barklie told whoever would listen, "Mr. Vansant's death was the most horrible I ever saw."

DETECTION AND CONCEALMENT

The sun was high as Gertrude Schuyler stepped into the surf of Atlantic City and splashed seawater on her bathing costume. She glanced back at her husband and eight-year-old daughter on the beach, and then she was in, a cool shock in the beginning, but presently she was accustomed to it. A typist employed in an office in Manhattan, Gertrude had porcelain white, city skin, and she glanced longingly at the warm, sun-bright sky, for a "ruddy sunburn" was coming into vogue.

If Gertrude was aware that north across Little Egg Inlet lay Long Beach Island, and that on the island was a small village with a few hotels, she did not know that a shark had killed a man there the day before, or that the shark was now stalking the coast. The story had yet to make the papers. When Gertrude Schuyler had boarded the shore train from New York City that morning, the papers were preoccupied with a different undersea predator—the *Deutschland*, the enormous German U-boat menacingly docked in Baltimore Harbor. In a world without radio or television, much of the news that summer traveled with traditional unhurried ease, by post and spoken word in local quarters.

In Beach Haven, Dr. Vansant made arrangements for his son's funeral, and the tragedy shadowed the bright July Fourth festivities at the Engleside Hotel. At the beach in front of the hotel, hundreds of heretofore carefree swimmers were afraid to go back in the water. But Beach Haven officials, perhaps to protect the tourist trade, cabled no alarm of the attack beyond the hotel. All along the 127-mile Atlantic coast of

New Jersey that Sunday, the first documented case in American history of a man taken as shark prey was attended by silence. From Cape May north to Atlantic Highlands, thousands of swimmers blissfully took to the beaches, unaware they shared the water with a rogue shark.

Gertrude Schuyler began to stroke along the coast, enjoying the freedom of a swim in shallow water. The surfmen (the term for lifeguards then) stood on the beach, coolly eyeing the horizon and sea and crowds as if by standing still they could somehow take it all in, eyes alert for unusual movement. The surfmen were assisted by athletic young volunteers who strutted about with spools on their belts containing five yards of stout rope to toss to distressed swimmers. The surfmen had their hands full that day: There were thousands of people in the water now, and the number would grow, by day's end, to fifty thousand.

Suddenly without warning an overpowering force pulled Gertrude Schuyler under. She was in the grip of something unimaginably strong, against which struggle was useless. She flailed her arms before they disappeared. Resurfacing for a moment, she made one panicked shout for help, and then all one could hear were the frightful screams of men and women whose worst nightmare of the beach was realized.

One of the surfmen must have seen her, because swiftly several surfmen and rescue volunteers rushed to the point where the water had whitened, their lifeboat splitting the waves.

Postcard from Atlantic City, New Jersey, circa 1910

A High Ball at Atlantic City, N.J.

A surfman as depicted in the *New York Herald*, July 9, 1916

Whether luck or divine assistance came to Gertrude Schuyler is not known, but in a moment she was free and in the arms of rescuers. Long minutes later she was back on the beach, coughing up seawater and accepting comfort from her husband and concerned strangers. Exciting plans for touring Atlantic City's amusements had given way to gratitude for being alive. It was a stunning if unflattering story for Gertrude to take back on the train: She had nearly drowned.

The pattern was disturbingly familiar to Atlantic City's surfmen. Eleven times that Sunday they heard screams for rescue; eleven times the surfmen and volunteers rushed into the water with ropes and pulled men and women to safety. Many bathers at the turn of the century didn't know how to swim, yet threw themselves into the currents and undertow to join the fad. Drownings were common.

Not until the next day, Monday, July third, was the existence of a dangerous sea creature on the shore publicly known. Readers had to turn deep inside the *Philadelphia Evening Bulletin* to learn of the death of the son of a prominent Philadelphia family two days earlier in a mysterious attack at sea. The same day, *The New York Times* devoted prominent headlines to local heroes at the shore over the holiday weekend—the men who'd rescued five passengers from a sinking pleasure boat off Manhattan Beach, and the surfmen who prevented eleven drownings in Atlantic City. On the last page of the *Times*, at the bottom of the page, was a small headline over a brief, four-paragraph story: "Dies After Attack by Fish." The two-day-old story portrayed the death at sea as a freak accident. What fish was capable of tearing a man to pieces the *Times* did not say.

Along the bottom of the night sea, the shark moved in cold depths unilluminated by the light of the moon. The shark had killed and failed to feed, and discipline and wariness ruled its every movement. The spoiled attack on a large mammal, the noisome counterattack by many other mammals, deepened its preternatural caution.

The great white possesses a large and complex brain, but the ability to reason is beyond it. "Reasoning implies the ability to integrate experience, forethought, rationality, learning . . . into a complex decision-making process," ichthyologist George Burgess says. "Sharks, like most animals, simply react in predetermined ways that, from an evolutionary standpoint, are clearly effective—or else they wouldn't be here any longer! That's why white sharks don't hold grudges, and don't spare women and children. . . ."

As the shark swam, tiny organs, distributed all along its body, constantly "tasted" the chemical composition and salinity of the ocean water. These sensors possessed cells analogous to the taste cells on a human tongue and sensed, now, lower salinity in the coastal waters. The shark was reading the dilution of coastal waters caused by the rains of June 1916, so torrential the *Ledger* lamented, "There cannot be much more rain left in Heaven." For eons, lower salinity had pointed the shark and its ancestors toward new hunting grounds, and so the big fish moved now toward prey.

Along with the shark's gifts of detection and concealment was the quality of anonymity, the gift of being unknown to man. By 1916, hundreds of men had been devoured by sharks. But sharks attacked far from cities and civilization. Shark attack was an otherworldly story swapped by sailors and fishermen, a tale seldom reaching beyond cabin or dock or the range of a man's last desperate cries. It was a story, when filtered to a city, that was scarcely believed.

Following the inlets, the shark moved along the thin, sandy coast of Long Beach Island. In several days the shark swept north where the barrier islands ended. There it began to hug the mainland for the first time. The inlets on the coast sang with life, with normal prey. But the juvenile great white was not behaving normally. Day and night, the water thrummed with mammals, a new and different quarry in unusual abundance. Along the beaches of the Jersey Shore that summer was perhaps the largest number of human beings in the water in any era to date.

THE DISTANCE SWIMMERS

The New Essex and Sussex Hotel spread out to occupy an entire seaside block of Spring Lake, forty-five miles up the coast from Beach Haven. Old Glory fluttered high from four turrets above the soaring portico. In the first week of July 1916, uniformed porters attended the parade of chauffeured Pierce Arrows arriving from New York, Texas, the South, and the Midwest to join the summer colony. By setting and architecture, the New Essex and

The New Essex and
Sussex Hotel

Sussex had announced itself an enclave of wealth and power in a bright and optimistic new century. And this, in fact, it was.

Many of the E & S's guests had read about the young man in Beach Haven who was attacked and killed the previous Saturday by a shark, and sharks were a subject of worrisome gossip and speculation. But the excitement subsided as longtime residents assured guests that sharks never attacked bathers on the Jersey coast. Some insisted that the details of Vansant's death had been fabricated by the newspapers, or grossly misunderstood, as the youth must have simply drowned. "The first accident of its kind recorded in the annals of the Jersey coast created considerable excitement," the *Asbury Park Press* reported, but "doubt as to the veracity of the dispatches from Beach Haven was frequently expressed."

On July 6, the newspapers declared it a fine beach day, made more precious by the rain predicted to arrive over the weekend. As the sun climbed that morning, bathers made their pilgrimage to the sea. On the broad, sandy beach, knots of children built sand castles, an activity being popularized by Lorenzo Harris, the one-armed sculptor from Philadelphia, who was molding "Neptune's Court" nearby.

By the proper mores of Spring Lake, women's bodies were draped in dark wool, and men covered up in black, two-piece bathing costumes. The male chest in 1916 was a scandalous zone prohibited from public view. Almost a century later, in the first worldwide study of great white attacks—covering 179 cases—nine of ten human victims wore gear or clothing that was dark: 74 percent were clad in black, 15 percent in blue. Thus, as they entered the waves in dark bathing costumes that July, swimmers were unknowingly appearing underwater in the coloration exhibited by many marine animals—the great white's chosen prey.

An advertisement for bathing suits in the *Philadelphia Press*, July 9, 1916

As the sun tipped toward afternoon, Robert W. Dowling, nineteen years old, stood on the beach and declared he was going to swim four miles straight out into the Atlantic, sharks be damned. Long-distance swimming being an amateur sport of the Edwardian wealthy, men and women would have taken the measure of the young man in a glance, then turned toward the horizon. It would be an impressive sight from shore, a story for a postcard or a letter home, something to witness. Robert Dowling had garnered headlines the previous summer, making a forty-mile swim around Manhattan Island. This new feat should not tax him, and the presence of a shark was not a true concern. And so Dowling swaggered to the line of the surf and plunged in. Soon he was as an arrow splitting the blue.

Not far south on the beach, Leonard Hill attracted no such attention. He was a wholesale druggist from New York City, treating his wife to a stay at the Essex and Sussex. He intended to swim straight out a quarter mile from the coast, then stroke five miles due south. If there were rogue waves about that day, Hill would be more likely to find them, but he was a strong swimmer and unafraid. Few people saw Leonard Hill as he gracefully turned in the water some distance from shore and, powerfully windmilling his arms, struck out in the direction of Beach Haven.

Both swimmers grew smaller on the horizon, dissolving finally in distant trails of white.

Off the coast, a tall fin divided the sea into segments, signaling the path of the huge fish. The fish moved with the precision and trajectory of an enormous bullet, a shot somehow fired in slow motion through the medium of the sea. Invisible lateral lines running down the length of its body recorded changing water pressure. They signaled its brain to adjust its fins. As it moved, it read the earth's magnetic field—or the electricity generated by ocean currents moving about the field—like an electromagnetic compass. It rode swells of water and magnetism and electricity as a sailor courses the wind.

The shark could see colors. It could see several feet out of the water, could have seen people in a small boat looking down at it if a vessel were circling over it, and now it noticed the light in the sky changing and slightly darkening like the water. The fish had traveled some fifty miles along the coast in five days, and it was hungry. It is not known how often it came near shore during those five days, explored bays and harbors, fed or failed to feed. But judging by its actions, its need to consume prey had become acute.

As the shark neared Spring Lake, sound ratcheted curiosity up toward urgency. The noises were deep, low-frequency sounds, bass notes beyond human perception: the noise emitted by a speared fish, thrashing about, or by a human being splashing in the water.

Dowling and Hill were far into the Atlantic by then, miles apart and miles from shore, unaware they had entered the tracking range of a great white.

The shark now turned its head slowly, side to side, letting water wash into its nostrils and out again. The horizontal balancing movement of the head allowed the shark to test a wide corridor of smell. Its nose was "thinking," and turning its head reflexively in the direction of the nostril that received the strongest smell, the fish proceeded that way. Like a hunting dog's, the shark's nasal cavity contains numerous folds to increase the surface area and number of olfactory sensors, but this nose was spectacularly more sensitive than a hunting dog's. Sharks can detect one part of blood in one million parts of water. A shark is even capable of responding to concentrations of fish extract of one part in ten billion.

To survive as a great white shark is extraordinarily difficult, so nature has supplied it with extraordinary weapons.

A quarter mile distant, the great white could smell its prey. It had entered an odor corridor, a wide swath of scent in the rough shape of an arrow, broad at the base and tapering to a point. The shark simply needed to follow the narrowing scent to its source.

The shark was in the water with them. This thought would soon come to both Dowling and Hill. Yet it is perhaps not surprising that both men were unafraid of the potential presence of a shark. The Edwardians were the first generation for whom the ocean had lost its terrors; the sea was a haven of leisure and entertainment. "We've forgotten what the ocean is," says George Burgess. "The ocean is a wilderness. We would never enter a forest wilderness without being aware of its dangers, its predators. Yet we think of the ocean as our giant backyard swimming pool."

On the Atlantic coast, sharks are constantly near shore, hunting and scavenging. Fly over Florida beaches in a helicopter or a small plane, Burgess says, and invariably you'll see them between the line of swimmers and the shore. The big shadows passing silently in four, six, nine feet of water, spying swimmers and moving on.

In the daylight hours of July 6, 1916, Robert W. Dowling swam unaware of the appraisal of him as potential prey. His movements were erratic, like a wounded fish's, yet the ocean was gentle and accommodating as he stroked four miles and soon climbed out of the sea to handshakes and applause. Farther south, Leonard Hill returned, too—to land, to safety, and to kudos of his own. Perhaps these long-distance swimmers were judged unpalatable or too large to attack. It is not known why the shark bypassed either man or precisely why it kept hunting humans, only that it did.

When Dowling and Hill received the news later of how close they had come to a man-eater, the endorphin euphoria of a long swim dissolved in chilled sweat. It is on record that both men immediately made new vacation plans. Separately, they vowed to abandon their careers as long-distance swimmers. Leonard Hill swore he'd never swim beyond the lifelines again. Dowling, the celebrity swimmer, was more emphatic. Of the two men, he had swum closer to the path of the shark, quite near it, there seemed no doubt. He swore he would never swim in the ocean again.

"Never again," he repeated. "At least, not here."

"HE'S A BIG FELLOW AND AWFUL HUNGRY"

Across Ocean Drive, men and women were returning from the beach for the afternoon siesta, and beneath the hum of roadsters along the coast road came the hissing and sighing of the waves, as if calling them back. Like clockwork, the hotel received the retreating bathers, porters and bellboys directing them to changing rooms near the elevators. The bathing costumes, smartly cleaned and ironed, would be returned to guests' rooms for tomorrow's swim. Meanwhile, no sandaled feet traversed the cavernous lobby, no seawater dripped across the endless Oriental rugs. Slowly, the hotel descended into afternoon slumber.

Strolling through the lobby with the swagger of an athlete was a young man, blond and muscular, striking beyond the sameness of his hotel uniform. Charles Bruder, the bell captain, ran his staff with crisp precision, creating the illusion that the hotel was a smoothly oiled machine. Yet Bruder was young; running the bell staff could not absorb all his energy. So during the somnolent hours of a Thursday afternoon, the bell captain saw a moment to escape from his duties for a brief swim.

As he headed down to the ocean, Bruder convinced Henry Nolan, the elevator runner, to break for a swim, and granted several bellhops time off to join them. The bell captain swam every day with his coworkers, but on July 6 he was especially eager for witnesses. Two other men had stolen his glory that afternoon. Robert Dowling and Leonard Hill were the talk of the hotel after their marathon swims, and Bruder was eager to reclaim his place as the beach's star. He also was eager to back up his boasts that he had swum many times with

Lobby of the Essex and
Sussex Hotel

large sharks off the coast of California and was unafraid of them. That morning the bellhops had been discussing the death of Charles Vansant. Bruder, with characteristic cockiness, mocked the newspaper accounts and insisted Vansant could not have been killed by a shark.

According to Bruder, sharks were large and scary-looking, but entirely harmless.

Bruder had worked the previous year at a hotel near Los Angeles, and on days off had gone swimming off Catalina Island, twenty miles off the coast. With his characteristic bravado, Bruder had swum among schools of five-foot leopard sharks and emerged, to the admiration of onlookers, unscathed. But Bruder could not have known that the leopard is considered sluggish for a shark and is quite harmless to humans, preferring fish, fish eggs, crustaceans, and worms. The leopard shark is an easy snack for a great white, often swallowed whole.

With dispatch that afternoon in Spring Lake, Bruder hustled to the bathhouses. He would not have time to match Dowling's four-mile trek, but he planned a fast, powerful swim and a quick return to the hotel. While the crowds had left the water to rest for evening, dozens of people remained on the sands, and the bell captain approaching the edge of the sea drew attention. Bruder's reputation was established: He put on a good show in the water.

Before he entered the water, Bruder stopped to talk with Captain George White and Christopher Anderson, of the lifesaving station, about the Philadelphia man who had supposedly been killed by a shark. Bruder repeated that "he was not afraid of sharks," according to the *New York Herald*.

Perhaps the bellhops, given their earlier discussions about Vansant, hesitated at the lip of the sea, but as Bruder charged in, they, too, entered the surf in a burst of noisy camaraderie. With a slow, powerful crawl, Charles Bruder swam straight out from shore—the same direction Dowling had swum earlier that afternoon. White and Anderson didn't budge as Bruder dipped his head under the safety ropes; he was a strong swimmer and often swam beyond the lifelines.

Ocean swimmers on the
Jersey Shore, circa 1920

With surprising speed, Bruder was soon a thousand feet from shore, drawing murmurs and comments from observers on the beach. At a thousand feet he was still going as if racing a clock. Soon Bruder was a diminishing figure on the eastern horizon, his arms slicing through the waves.

As graceful as Bruder appeared from shore, his movements were sprawling, rough, almost obscenely graceless for a creature of the sea, his limbs thudding flat and hard on the surface, radiating erratic waves of sound. It was only natural that the shark, patrolling nearby, would decide to investigate. Through the murk of the darkening sea, the great white sped, trailing sonic waves, until it was close enough, within fifteen feet, to see plainly the source of the sounds.

Bruder was twelve hundred feet from shore. The water was over his head, but less than ten feet deep in the low tide. As the pale bottoms of Bruder's feet turned this way and that, they emitted a faint light in the gloom. His palms were small points of light, too, as he stroked his arms in a crawl, tiny flares wriggling up, down, and around, darting to the surface and plunging down. The whirl of light was imperceptibly dim to human eyes, but the shark's eyes have a heightened ability to distinguish an object from a contrasting background. No more than a dozen feet away, the shark's brain processed the flickering light as the movement of a fish.

Moving closer, beneath its prey, the shark had seen its quarry in full silhouette, etched by sunlight—outlined, in a glimpse that triggered both excitement and wariness, as not a school of fish but a mammal. After its struggle with Vansant and his rescuers, the shark had good reason to fear the large, slow coastal mammals. Yet perhaps Bruder's shape resembled a seal, and the shark considered an investigatory bite. The evidence suggests that the juvenile great white, driven by necessity or insanity, was deliberately stalking undesirable prey for which competition was scarce: human flesh. No sharks in history have been known to travel so far to locate and consume so much human flesh.

Something else about Bruder greatly appealed to the shark. He was alone—no one within hundreds of yards. Unlike the shark, for whom every movement is calculated for advantage in the struggle of life and death, the man swam with no protection, no attempt at concealment, no sense of urgency. Charles Bruder swam as if he were alone in the sea, as if he were invincible.

The great white's surprise attack was launched with overpowering force from behind. As the shark moved, its dark top reflected virtually no light. The denticles on its skin muted the whoosh of its movements as the shark rose, driven by the power of the great tail sweeping from side to side, like a scythe. Charles Bruder could not have heard the faint sucking rush of water not far beneath him. He couldn't have seen or heard what was hurtling from the murk at astonishing speed, jaws unhinging, widening, for the enormous first bite. It was the classic attack that no other creature in nature could make—a bomb from the depths.

History did not record Charles Bruder's thoughts or feelings as he experienced a surprise great white attack. Instead, the sea told his story. Guests on the beach in front of the Essex and Sussex suddenly saw a massive spray of water rising out of the ocean. As the plunging wall of water descended, a woman on the beach cried out, "The man in the red canoe is upset!" The surfmen White and Anderson shoved their small rescue rowboat into the water and began to row frantically while panicked shouts rang from the boardwalk and beach. As White and Anderson pulled closer, they saw that the "red canoe" was blood, spreading now in a wide circle. Rushing toward the red stain, they were suddenly greeted by the unimaginable sight of the bell captain pinwheeling above the surface of the sea with incredible force.

As the surfmen drew closer, the huge fish struck Bruder again and again. Finally, Bruder was pulled completely under. As White and Anderson's rescue boat entered the sea of blood, the bell captain somehow managed to lift his head above water and gasp, "A shark bit me." The surfmen lowered an oar, and Bruder, with tremendous effort, lifted himself onto the gunwales, then collapsed, clinging helplessly to the side of the boat. Quickly, White and Anderson grabbed Bruder under the arms and hoisted him into the lifeboat. The surfmen, their strength fueled by urgency, were surprised how easy it was to lift the husky bell captain to safety. Laying him carefully on the bottom of the boat, the reason was immediately evident: There was little of Bruder left to lift. In a glance, White and Anderson noted "the loss of both of his feet." The surfmen were covered with blood.

While one surfman pulled the oars of the boat, the other tried desperately to stop the bleeding from both Bruder's legs by ripping off his shirt to cobble together makeshift tourniquets. Blood continued to pump copiously, soaking the boat. There was little time, but Bruder was still conscious.

According to the *New York Herald*, Bruder described the attack to the surfmen in the boat. "He was a big gray fellow, and as rough as sandpaper. I didn't see him until after he struck me the first time. He cut me here in the side, and his belly was so rough it bruised my face and arms. That was when I yelled the first time. I thought he had gone on, but he only turned and shot back at me [and] . . . snipped my left leg off. . . . He yanked me clear under before he let go. . . . He came back at me again . . . and shook me like a terrier shakes a rat. But he let go while I was calling, then suddenly . . . took off the other leg. He's a big fellow and awful hungry."

Perhaps the story was embellished by the *Herald*, but whatever Bruder said, White and Anderson listened wide-eyed as they rowed their wounded friend to shore, trying to hurry yet make him as comfortable as possible. As the lifeboat surged through the waves, Charles Bruder closed his eyes and lost consciousness.

OUT OF THE WATER

Mrs. George W. Childs of Philadelphia was ensconced in a high and lovely suite at the Essex and Sussex, with fine views of the ocean. At two-thirty that afternoon, the grande dame had settled into her room for a respite before the social requirements of evening when she heard, with a keen acuity for her age, disturbing noises floating through the windows over the sea. Mrs. Childs called to her maid to bring the field glasses and stepped out on her private balcony. Scanning south of the hotel, Mrs. Childs saw a small boat had breached the shore. Two men—in the bathing costumes of surfmen—lifted a man out of the boat and set him down on the sands. Mrs. Childs's view was partially obscured by the shifting crowd, but presently she saw, to her astonishment, that the man lying on the beach was covered with blood. On either side of the fallen man, mothers hurried children out of the water as if it were boiling. On the sands, women in long dresses swooned. Men rushed to assist them. From her distant balcony the grande dame heard, as if from the wind and sea itself, faint but unmistakable cries of "Shark!" She had seen all she needed, and heard quite enough.

Putting down the field glasses, Mrs. Childs rushed for the telephone and dialed the hotel office. F. T. Keating, assistant manager of the hotel, picked up. Keating, alarmed, went straight to the hotel manager, David B. Plumer, who—without time to consider the uniqueness of the situation—put into motion the first coastwide shark alarm in the history of the United States. Plumer instructed

Keating to call every physician booked in the hotel or anywhere in Spring Lake. Moving urgently to the E & S switchboard, he ordered the operators to notify every "central" operator on the north and central coast. Within minutes, the E & S operators reached every major hotel on New Jersey's Gold Coast, from Atlantic Highlands, sixteen miles north, to Point Pleasant, six miles south.

For the first time in memory along the East Coast of the United States, a tranquil beach day was interrupted by surfmen running to the edge of the sea to frantically wave swimmers out of the water; by bathers thrashing and stumbling madly to shore for reasons that were urgent if not clear. Within half an hour, thousands of bathers fled more than thirty miles of beaches in a shark panic without precedent.

Within minutes, Drs. William W. Trout and A. Cornell pressed through the small crowd that had gathered around the body in the wet sand. The bell captain lay on his back in a welter of blood that was already crusting and drying on his bathing costume and diffusing on the sand. Trout and Cornell summoned their full professional composure, but jellyfish stings, crab pinches, and sunburn were the usual toll of the beach. In their combined years, the physicians had not seen such wounds from an animal attack. Bruder's left leg was bitten off clear above the knee; his right leg, just below the knee, was gone. A huge gouge was ripped from his torso, the wound edged with large teeth marks. The bell captain was already dead from massive blood loss. There was nothing to do but arrange for the body to be taken to autopsy and to calm the crowd.

Facing gasps and muffled sobs, Trout and Cornell were relieved to see the large, loose-limbed figure of Dr. William G. Schauffler, the governor's staff physician and surgeon of the New Jersey National Guard, ambling across the sands. As Dr. Schauffler kneeled to inspect Bruder's

Boy, Legs Bitten Off by Shark, Dies After Fight in the Surf

Life Guards Go to Rescue of Charles Bruder, Far Off Shore in Waters Near Spring Lake, N. J., but He Succumbs After Describing Vicious Attack.

[SPECIAL DESPATCH TO THE HERALD.]

SPRING LAKE, N. J., Thursday.—A shark bit both legs off a boy swimming in the surf here this afternoon and in its vicious strokes otherwise wounded him so that he died soon after being taken ashore. He lived long enough, however, to tell a remarkable story of his encounter.

A Philadelphia man was killed by a shark off Beach Haven, near Atlantic City, about a week ago. Those are the only appearances "man-eating" sharks have made in those waters. There always have been plenty of "blue nose" sharks, but they have been considered harmless.

The killing of Charles Bruder this afternoon has caused intense excitement along the coast, and the resort owners fear that much damage will result to their business unless speedy steps are taken to rid the waters of the danger. With that end in view patrols already have been established by launches which make a loud exhaust noise. Those small craft have been assigned to run up and down the coast from 100 to 500 yards off shore, it being believed their noise will frighten the sharks away.

Bruder, seventeen years old, was a bell boy in the new Essex and Sussex Hotel here. He was a very strong swimmer and always went far out beyond the life lines. As he entered the water to-day he stopped and talked with Captain White and Christopher Anderson, of the life saving station, about the Philadelphia man who had been killed by a shark. He said he was not afraid of sharks; that off Catalina Island, California, he had seen many and they always fled from bathers.

The boy was about 100 yards off shore when Captain White heard him cry for aid. He saw him go under the water twice and then come up, and those two times under the water proved to be when the shark took off the legs, one at a time.

Captain White and Anderson launched a boat quickly and ran out to where Bruder was trying to keep himself afloat. The water about him was stained a deep crimson and the life guards knew what had happened. They hauled the boy into the boat and hurried back to shore. On the way Bruder said:—

"He was a big gray fellow, and as rough as sandpaper. I didn't see him until after he struck me the first time. He cut me here in the side, and his belly was so rough it bruised my face and arms.

"That was when I yelled the first time. I thought he had gone on, but he only turned and shot back at me. That time he snipped my left leg off, just below the knee. He yanked me clear under before he let go. I had hardly reached the surface when he came back at me again. That time he bit me here in the side, an awful blow, and he shook me like a terrier shakes a rat. But he let go while I was calling, then suddenly struck at me again and that time took off the other leg. He's a big fellow and awful hungry."

Bruder tried to say more, but he became too weak and he died while tourniquets were being twisted about his legs.

Captain White and other men who have been along the coast here most of their lives said to-night there was very little danger from such sharks, except to the strong swimmers who go far out from shore. No matter how hungry or vicious a shark may be he never will approach a group of bathers and never has been known to venture nearer than a hundred yards to the shore.

Bruder's home was in Switzerland. He came here only a few weeks ago when the Essex and Sussex was opened and is not known to have any relatives in this country.

New York Herald, page one, July 7, 1916

corpse, a troubled expression creased his youthful features. Schauffler's appraisal was that of a doctor who was also a skilled fisherman. Later, Schauffler filed the first detailed medical report of a shark attack victim in the United States. "The left foot was missing as well as the lower end of the tibia and fibula," he wrote. "The leg bone was denuded of flesh from a point halfway below the knee. There was a deep gash above the left knee, which penetrated to the bone. On the right side of the abdomen low down, a piece of flesh as big as a man's fist was missing. There is not the slightest doubt that a man-eating shark inflicted the injuries."

Schauffler's report anticipated the classic study of shark attack victims by South African doctors Davies and Campbell half a century later. In the terminology of Davies and Campbell, Bruder suffered the severest shark-inflicted injury possible, a grade one. Had he suffered the same attack in the early twenty-first century, he still would have died, even with instant and advanced medical response.

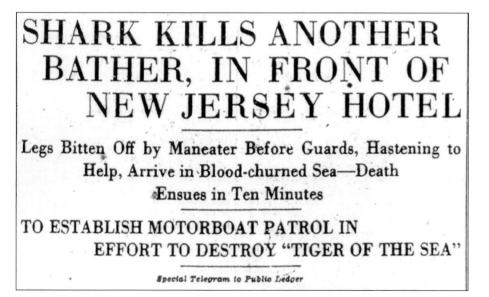

SHARK KILLS ANOTHER BATHER, IN FRONT OF NEW JERSEY HOTEL

Legs Bitten Off by Maneater Before Guards, Hastening to Help, Arrive in Blood-churned Sea—Death Ensues in Ten Minutes

TO ESTABLISH MOTORBOAT PATROL IN EFFORT TO DESTROY "TIGER OF THE SEA"

Special Telegram to Public Ledger

Philadelphia Public Ledger,
July 7, 1916

Philadelphia Public Ledger,
July 8, 1916

As Schauffler rose from beside Bruder's body, he was convinced of what had to be done. He was already forming plans to organize a patrol—armed men and a fleet of boats—to protect bathers and capture and kill the shark. The shark, he believed, was a confirmed man-eater, a large and deranged animal that would continue to threaten swimmers until it was destroyed.

"The news that the man had been killed by a shark spread rapidly through the resort, and many persons were so overcome by the horror of Bruder's death that they had to be assisted to their rooms," *The New York Times* reported. "Swimmers hurried out of the water and couldn't be induced to return." With the coming of twilight, local residents were drawn irresistibly to the hotel to make sense of the tragedy, but sense dissolved in a babel of opinion. Old-time fishermen insisted a shark attack was too far-fetched to believe, that swordfish, giant sea turtles, and big mackerel were more likely man-killers than a shark. Townfolk recalled, with knotted stomachs, the shark caught by a Spring Lake fisherman in 1913. In the fish's stomach was the foot of an unidentified woman, the foot still encased in a fashionable tan shoe. But it was concluded then that the shark had scavenged the body of a drowned woman. Sharks were considered too timid to threaten a live human being.

Late on the afternoon Charles Bruder died, a balding man with a bemused professorial air, thin and ruddy as a stalk of rhubarb, strolled through the lobby of the Essex and Sussex. John Treadwell Nichols was impressively tall, with a wry manner that made him appear older than his thirty-three years. There was about his wide-set eyes and cheekbones a certain fishlike quality that seemed entirely appropriate, as he was one of the most distinguished ichthyologists of the day. Dr. Nichols had been rousted from his specimen-crowded basement

office at the American Museum of Natural History in New York City to commence what would be the first scientific investigation of a man killed by a fish in American history.

But Dr. Nichols was not inclined to think of it as a shark-attack inquiry. Such attacks on man were rare, if not nonexistent. Nichols had examined the torn and badly bitten body of Charles Bruder, restraining his sympathy for the young man, to objectively consider the wounds as the quite natural acts of a fish or mammal species. But which one?

Nichols then held a small conference with reporters in Spring Lake to discuss his findings. To the surprise of the newspapermen, the ichthyologist declared it was not a shark that had killed the young man. Dr. Nichols's leading suspect was *Orcinus orca*, the killer whale. Bruder's legs had been torn off in dull, jagged cuts, wounds that recalled to Nichols the enormous, blunt, conical teeth with which the orca rips the lips and tongues from the great whales.

Nichols's choice in 1916 was not surprising. Since antiquity, the killer whale had been reputed to be a man-eater, a voracious, merciless predator that killed everything that lived in the sea. Spanish whalers in the eighteenth century christened the species "killer whale" after witnessing schools of orca descending upon and killing other whales, like a pack of wolves. It was only in the 1960s and '70s, after killer whales were trained to perform at Sea World, that scientists began to appreciate the orca as the smartest member of the dolphin family, and to accept the fact that there are no documented cases of an orca ever killing a man.

The killer whale, Nichols told reporters in Spring Lake, was "commonly thirty feet long," with "short, stumpy teeth which are very efficacious in dragging things under the surface"—which explained why Bruder was repeatedly pulled beneath the waves. The orca kills the giant blue whale, the largest creature on earth, Dr. Nichols pointed out, and could easily destroy a man if it chose. "It is not settled that the killer whale attacks humans," concluded *The New York Times*, "but Mr. Nichols thought there was as much reason to suppose it was a killer whale as to suppose it was a shark."

Blue Shark, Slayer of Two Bathers.

This is the type of shark supposed to have killed Charles E. Vansant and Charles Bruder on the New Jersey coast within a week. Fish of this family are often 30 to 40 feet long. They usually do not attack man, but live chiefly on shellfish and fish. Both victims on the Jersey shore were first disabled by bites on the legs.

Philadelphia Press,
July 8, 1916

ARRIVAL OF A MAN-EATER

Far from shore the great white moved into deeper waters, likely doing what it always did: swimming steadily forward, dorsal fin high, searching for the next meal. All of Charles Bruder would certainly have sated the shark, but the legs left it hungry, imparted slightly more urgency to the search that never ended. If the attack on Bruder taught it anything, it was that the mammals of the coast were vulnerable but not easy prey.

The great white had been frightened off by White and Anderson's lifeboat, which it perceived as a bigger predator, or it was simply spooked by a large foreign object, which sharks hastily avoid. Had the fish been mature, eighteen feet and one and a half tons, neither boats nor men, oars nor bullets would have stopped the feeding.

Now the great white moved off the coast of Spring Lake, deeply irritated, electric with hunger. To a great white, a man is a bony, unpalatable, low-fat choice, distressingly muscular. Enormous quantities of fat, scientists believe, fuel the great white's energy needs. The preference is striking: Whites feeding on a whale carcass have been witnessed carefully stripping away the blubbery layers.

Survival for a young white in the mid-Atlantic was precarious. Absent the fatty prey available on the West Coast—sea lions, elephant seals—the shark subsisted mostly on large fish such as rake and cod and red drum. As it grew larger than ten feet, the mid-Atlantic offered porpoises, sea turtles, and harbor seals, still extant off New Jersey in the first part of the century. But big, blubbery prey was scarce.

Denied its usual diet, the great white would have turned to the lesser prey items it consumes as the need arises. Exactly what the great white eats in an emergency is a mystery ichthyologists solved by the late twentieth century: whatever it wishes. The giant fish devours the living and the dead and the inanimate. Bottles, tin cans, cuckoo clocks, truck tires, a whole sheep, an intact Newfoundland dog with its collar on, have all been taken from the stomach of whites. In the days when animal carcasses were thrown in the ocean, boars, pigs, the head of a horse, a whole horse, and the entire skin of a buffalo found their way into the stomachs of great white sharks. Almost anything is within the reach of a mouth that takes fifty pounds in a single bite.

The white shark's preference for pinnipeds, fish, and other sea creatures over human flesh is documented. Burgess's worldwide study of white attacks shows that in the majority of the 179 attacks—56.8 percent of the cases—human victims received only a single bite and were "spit out." Some shark biologists believe humans resemble seals and, when proven to be impostors, are spit out; others insist humans are rejected as insufficiently fatty. Burgess interprets the shark's "bite and spit" behavior differently. The white shark's attacks on humans parallel its attacks on sea creatures—after the first strike it circles around, giving the prey time to bleed out.

According to George Burgess, the shark bit and spit not because its human victim was unpalatable, but because it simply ceased its attack:

> It wasn't given an opportunity for a second bite. We have enough deaths and consumptions in the Attack File to know a white shark will happily consume a human being if it wants to. But because of our brain and social structure, a person grabbed by a white shark has a very good chance of getting to a boat, getting on a surfboard, having a swimming buddy help him escape the water. The poor sea lion

New York World,
July 8, 1916

doesn't have those assets. If humans were unpalatable we wouldn't have bodies disappearing and consumed.

As the sun rounded over the ocean on Friday, July 7, at Spring Lake, a small squadron of boats split the shallows, gunning loud motorboat engines and trailing diluted crimson pools of animal blood. On the prows of the boats stood groups of men, long rifles pointed down toward the water and harpoons angled high against the delicate blue sky. Roped to the boats were chunks of lamb slaughtered by the butcher that morning, bait for the man-eater. Dr. Schauffler had organized the patrol to catch and kill the shark, and also to protect bathers, so those who wished could swim with peace of mind. Yet before long young men, one at a time, left the water, returning to the hotel or the pool at the Bath and Tennis Club. Shortly, the line of blue-green breakers rolled in uninterrupted, and the beach at Spring Lake was bereft, for the first summer day in many years, of human presence.

The bell captain would be buried the next morning in nearby Manasquan, and the management of the E & S vowed to cover all expenses, as if by doing the right thing—and doing it quickly—the hotel and its guests could put the tragedy behind them. Word had reached the hotel that Asbury Park and towns up and down the coast were barricading their beaches from a man-eating shark.

By midmorning, a commotion swept the lobby of the E & S as colonists crowded around copies of the day's *New York Times*, smudging their fingers with ink as they passed around the broadsheet pages. "Shark Kills Bather Off New Jersey Beach," the front page blared. "Bites Off Both Legs of a Young Swimmer. Guards Find Him Dying. Women Are Panic-stricken as Mutilated Body Is Brought Ashore." Even the habitually restrained *Times* could not report the arrival of a man-eating shark without sensation. There was no other way to tell the story. Dispatches by *Times* correspondents from the Battle of the Somme and the Russian front and the British sinking of twenty-one German ships seemed somehow tame and distant in comparison. With its headlines and stories of July 7, 1916, the *Times* introduced the great white shark to American culture as a source of general fear, the twentieth-century sea monster. As guests folded back the front page, the previous night's bold assertions that a shark could not have killed Bruder evaporated in the daylight. Some guests locked themselves in their rooms, others simply packed to leave. It was as if the horrors of the previous day, stamped in newsprint, could no longer be denied.

Yet the history of shark attack is footnoted by denial, and Spring Lake, perhaps inevitably, was opposed to such an alarming view. Some Spring Lake residents and fishermen stubbornly continued to claim that there were far more likely man-killers than sharks. They swapped stories of giant mackerels and huge, swift swordfish that could run a man through with their long, steel-hard blades.

Whatever was out there concealed by the waves, for the first time in American history people en masse were afraid to enter the water. The four hundred to five hundred bathers who swam in the waters off the South Pavilion on Thursday dwindled on Friday to half a dozen brave souls drifting in and out of the surf. Finally, the surf emptied for good.

That afternoon, the sounds of distant, muffled gunshots reached the hotel, followed by an anxious account from the surfmen on the water's edge. A large shark had been spotted perilously close to the beach. The armed men of the shark patrol had raised their rifles and opened fire across the waves, shooting at a large fin. The fish eluded the spray of bullets and, apparently frightened, disappeared out to sea.

Bathers Are Cautious in the Surf These Days

GUARD ATTACKS
SHARK WITH OAR
FISH ESCAPES

Asbury Park Patrol Boat Beats
Off 15-foot Monster Near
Bathing Beach.

PROTECTED BY NETS

Special Despatch to "The Press."
Asbury Park, N. J., July 8—A shark, believed to be at least fifteen feet long, was sighted off the Asbury Avenue bathing grounds to-day and caused much excitement. Lifeguard Benjamin Everingham, who observed the big fish from his patrol boat, gave chase and struck the monster twice with an oar, but it made off to sea.

Bathing was prohibited at the Asbury Avenue grounds, and all others except Third and Fourth Avenues, where the grounds are enclosed with a heavy steel net. The motor boat patrol is doing efficient work along the coast and beach guards are confident that if bathers are

CONTINUED ON PAGE 2, COLUMN 1

BEACH HAVEN TO
SPREAD GREAT NET

Resort Will at Once Protect Its
Bathers Against Invasion
of Sharks.

RUSSIANS TAKE
MORE TOWNS IN
NEW ADVANCE

3600 Prisoners Taken in Day's
Fighting Along Far-Flung
Battle Line.

SOME TRENCHES LOST

Petrograd, July 8—The Russians have pressed back the Germans farther in the sector west of Czartorysk, occupying several more towns.

Capture of the villages of Dolrysa and Grualatyn was announced to-night by the War Office. Two thousand prisoners were taken yesterday.

Philadelphia Press, page one,
July 9, 1916

MYTHS OF ANTIQUITY

Forty-five miles north of Spring Lake, New York City was a sea of buildings. Looming over Broadway was the tallest building in the world, the fifty-eight-story Woolworth Building. Everything in New York seemed new and modern in 1916. Penn Station and Grand Central, Gimbel's and Ebbets Field, were all new to the feverish teens. At the Biograph Theater, D. W. Griffith launched the motion picture industry; Picasso, Matisse, and Picabia introduced modern art at the Armory Show.

Rising over the Upper West Side like a castle, the American Museum of Natural History was another icon of the new, for under its ten-acre roof the museum had mounted the most painstaking effort in the modern world to illuminate the shadowy myths of the past with the lamp of scientific investigation.

Late that July afternoon, a group of newspapermen presented themselves at the grand entrance of the museum and were dispatched to the office of the director of the museum and head of the scientific staff, Dr. Frederic Augustus Lucas.

Dr. Lucas was one of the preeminent scientists and museum men in the world, an authority in the fields of taxidermy, osteology (the study of bones), geology, and comparative anatomy. After twenty years as a curator at the Smithsonian in Washington, D.C., he had been appointed director of the American Museum in 1911. At Lucas's direction, the museum mounted the expeditions of many of the world's greatest botanists, anthropologists, and explorers. It dispatched Carl E. Akeley and Roosevelt to Africa and Peary to the North Pole.

Dr. Frederic Augustus Lucas

Dr. Lucas had also studied shark attacks for years, an endeavor that earned him the reputation of being the scientific community's reigning shark expert. It was Lucas who had sent John T. Nichols, one of his brightest assistants, to investigate the death of Charles Bruder in Spring Lake. But Nichols suspected a killer whale, while the newspapermen, and the public at large, were obsessed with the idea of a man-eating shark—a subject that, to the press's lament, no other men of science seemed to know much about. No less an authority than *The New York Times*—already the undisputed newspaper authority on matters of science—had declared Frederic Augustus Lucas "the greatest shark expert of this century."

The hullabaloo over a man supposedly killed by a shark in Spring Lake reminded him of the uproar over the "giant blob" that had washed ashore on Anastasia Island, Florida, in November 1896, causing an international sensation over the "Florida sea monster." Then, too, Dr. Lucas was required to step in and disappoint the masses with scientific fact, identifying the "blob" as no more than decayed whale blubber.

A disciplined and orderly man, he grew weary that week as newspapermen interrupted him with queries about the young man supposedly killed by a shark. What kind of shark was responsible? Are sharks man-eaters? Should swimmers be afraid? The names and faces of the men from the *Post* and *Times*, the *Herald* and *World*, the *Journal* and *Inquirer* and *Bulletin*, were different, but the questions were endlessly the same.

The director could imagine few myths as archaic and misguided as the myth of the sea monster, and particularly the weak-minded belief in a man-eating shark. The man-eating shark was a hysterical product of the myths of antiquity. Such a creature, as far as Dr. Lucas's thirty years of personal scientific investigations could determine, simply did not exist, or most certainly not in New York or New Jersey waters.

Asked by the New York press to comment on Bruder's death, Dr. Lucas was adamant to the point of finality that sharks were not capable of inflicting serious injury to man. Those who believed a shark had killed Charles Bruder, Lucas declared, had made one of the commonest errors in such cases, "that the shark bit off the man's leg as though it were a carrot." Such a feat was not possible, Lucas said, and the mere statement "shows that the maker or writer of it had little idea of the strength of the apparatus needed to perform such an amputation." Lucas described the common sense behind his theory. "The next time the reader carves a leg of lamb, let him speculate on the power required to sever this at one stroke—and the bones of a sheep are much lighter than those of a man. Moreover, a shark, popular belief to the contrary notwithstanding, is not particularly strong in the jaws."

As evidence, Dr. Lucas noted that his protégé, Robert Cushman Murphy, during an expedition to South Georgia Island, witnessed "the difficulty of sharks in tearing meat from the carcass of a whale." And Lucas recalled his own "disappointment at witnessing the efforts of a twelve-foot shark to cut a chunk out of a sea lion. The sea lion had been dead a week and was supposedly tender, but the shark tugged and thrashed and made a great to-do over each mouthful."

Given the weakness of even the largest sharks' jaws, Lucas reasoned, a shark was not capable of biting cleanly through the bone and therefore could not have been the animal that bit off Charles Bruder's legs. What animal was capable of the attack, Dr. Lucas couldn't say, but "certainly no shark recorded as having been taken in these waters could possibly perform such an act." According to Lucas, the best scientific data concerning the question of the East Coast shark attack remained the uncollected reward for the wager Hermann Oelrichs made in 1891. Twenty-five years had substantiated the tycoon's position, Lucas concluded, that there was "practically no danger of an attack . . . about our coasts."

A LONG-RANGE CRUISING ROGUE

As the motorboats rumbled and bloodied the waters of Spring Lake, not far offshore the great white swam with growing urgency. It had hunted with success, and prey was very close now, abundant prey; it could sense it with numerous electrical, sonic, and olfactory systems. Its lateral lines tingled with the distant vibration of motorboat engines. Molecules of blood in the water, carried on currents from miles away, moved in and out of the shark's flapped nostrils, firing its cerebellum to adjust its fins for a new direction. As the shark haunted the coast that afternoon, the men of New Jersey were growing edgy enough to shoot at anything that swam. It is likely the rogue great white was among the targets that the Spring Lake patrol fired at, for there is compelling evidence that it remained in the area after killing Bruder.

There is scant science on the matter of a rogue shark, a deliberate man-eater, while skepticism persists that such a creature exists. As people are not a regular prey for sharks, a purposeful hunter of humans must be injured, crazed, aberrant. Furthermore, an oceanic "serial killer" is nearly impossible to catch and convict, its work concealed, the evidence eradicated by the enclosing sea. But the late Dr. Sir Victor Coppleson, a distinguished Australian surgeon knighted by the queen, tracked the global movements of rogues across the twentieth century, beginning in 1922, when he began treating shark bites as a young doctor at St. Vincent's Hospital in Sydney. In 1933, Coppleson coined the term "rogue shark" in *The Medical Journal of Australia*. "A rogue shark," he wrote, "if the theory is correct, and evidence appears to prove it to the hilt—like the man-eating tiger, is a killer which, having experienced the deadly sport of killing or mauling a human, goes in search of similar game."

Rogue attacks began, Coppleson believed, with the rising popularity of beaches for recreational use at the turn of the century. Coppleson's base for investigation was Sydney, where rogue attacks were unknown until the sport of surfing arrived in 1919. Then, on February 4, 1922, Milton Coughlan, a surfman, was "cracking a few waves" on Coogee Beach when a large shark "struck with such terrific force that he was lifted from the water," whereupon a crowd watched a large pair of jaws snap off Coughlan's arm. He died shortly afterward at a local hospital. Coppleson suspected a pattern when, less than a month later, twenty-one-year-old Mervyn Gannon was struck and killed at the same beach. During the next three years, Nita Derritt lost both legs in a shark attack, and Jack Dagworthy lost a leg when a shark leapt out of the water at him, mouth agape. The work of a single deranged shark, Coppleson concluded in such cases, was the only logical explanation. It seemed to him far-fetched to believe that a beach swimming area, free from shark attack for decades, would suddenly be invaded by groups of man-eating sharks, then, just as suddenly, be free of attack for years to come. Often, the "rogue series"—a reign of terror lasting several days or years—ended when a single man-eater was captured.

In twenty-five years, Coppleson dis-covered the work of rogue sharks all over the world. In December 1957, in Durban, South Africa, during the three weeks known as Black December, three swimmers were killed, one was severely mauled, and another lost a leg. In San Juan, Puerto Rico, in the 1920s, he investigated five attacks on the same beach during three years, including that of an American schoolteacher who died almost instantly as a shark removed most of her hip, thigh, and related bones in a single bite, and that of a Professor Winslow, found with both arms and legs almost severed from his body, his hands gone. In Africa and Australia in the 1950s, Coppleson's theory was useful to people seeking an understanding of shark attacks, and led to the erection of shark nets to combat rogues. Only in the United States, where "writers for many years . . . have labeled most stories of shark attacks on humans as 'fish yarns,' were scientists skeptical," Coppleson found. Such skepticism was ironic, since in Coppleson's research, the United States trailed only Australia and Africa in shark attacks, and "one of the most remarkable series of shark attacks in world history" occurred on its Atlantic coast, in New Jersey, in 1916. The New Jersey case was one of a number that supported Coppleson's contention, "as fantastic as it may seem," that a rogue shark can strike at distances of sixty to eighty miles apart over several days or weeks. In fact, the Jersey shark was "the classic example of . . . a long-range cruising rogue."

Coppleson believed that he was so expert in profiling the tendencies of rogue sharks that he was able to predict days in advance when a man-eater would strike. When a shark attacking dogs near Botany Bay was mentioned in the *Sydney Morning Herald* in early January 1940, Coppleson later regretted not writing a letter to the editor to say that it fit the profile of a rogue. A large shark that appeared near a beach or harbor, "acting savagely, snapping fish from lines, tearing nets, and attacking dogs," charging boats or attacking anything in sight, was an incipient man-eater. On January 23, a thirteen-year-old boy, Maxwell Farrin, was killed by a shark near Botany Bay. The next day Coppleson published his letter advising capture of the shark and warning swimmers to be cautious, for "on the rogue shark theory it would strike again." John William Eke, fifty-five, didn't heed the warning, and eleven days later, four hundred yards from the Farrin attack, he lost his life to a shark.

Scientists in 1916 were ignorant of Coppleson's theory (it would not be published for another forty years). And by the twenty-first century, Coppleson's theory was widely dismissed by scientists. Yet the rogue theory gave shark-stricken coasts in the mid–twentieth century some grasp, some understanding, of the apex predator. Cluster attacks can now sometimes be explained by changes in coastal water temperature that draw sharks to beach areas when swimmers are in the water. In 1916, there was no such awareness. As the shark moved off the coast of Spring Lake and Asbury Park on July 7, 1916, there was no clue that it was escalating toward a series of attacks unprecedented in two thousand years of shark attacks on man. Many years later, Coppleson, in his exhaustive if anecdotal survey, concluded with some surprise that none of the fabled huge "white pointers" of Australia had ever traveled as widely to kill as many human beings, nor had any "ever shown the ferocity of the 'mad shark' of New Jersey in July 1916."

THE SHARK SCARE

His broad back to the sun, Benjamin Everingham dipped the oars of a small rowboat into the listless gray sea and pulled. He was fifty feet beyond the ropes at the Asbury Avenue beach, moving parallel to the coast. As the boat coasted, he looked toward the horizon, squinting for a fin, and, seeing nothing, he put his head down and pulled again. It was after eleven in the morning and the mild weather was a surprise. Mindful of the gift of a clear day, the summer people in the hotels and boardinghouses crowded the beaches early that Saturday.

The *Asbury Park Press* sang with reassuring headlines: "Will Assure Absolute Safety to Bathers. . . . Asbury Park Bathing Grounds All to Be Surrounded by Wire." A heavy, close-meshed wire netting, used for fishing but thought to be strong enough to keep out sharks, had been installed the day before at the Fourth Avenue beach from sea bottom to the high-tide level. Work hadn't started at Asbury Avenue yet. The beach was open to the sea, thus Everingham's assignment to row along the coast and keep an eye out for sharks.

Everingham was captain of the surfmen for the resort city, but by all accounts he was taking his assignment that day lightly. He was skeptical of reports that a shark had killed a man on Thursday in Spring Lake, four miles south. Fishermen in Asbury Park were saying it must have been a freak big mackerel or swordfish, and in any case, as an old-time seaman had said in the *Press*, "Such an accident is not apt to happen again in a thousand years." Instructed to carry a rifle and ax on his shark patrol to protect the bathers, Everingham hadn't bothered.

At a quarter to noon, when he turned toward the horizon, he saw a gray fin cutting the low waves. In an instant he recognized it as a large shark. It seemed to be fully eight feet long, and it was bearing directly for his boat. Just as the shark was about to strike his boat, the surfman stood and "lifted one of the oars from its lock and struck viciously at the slimy sea monster." Stricken, the creature turned sideways as if to flee, whereupon Everingham swung the oar and struck the big fish again, "and with a swirling of the waters the shark turned and shot out to sea."

Crowds watching from the beach and a nearby fishing pier were puzzled as they saw Everingham standing up in his boat, striking the surface of the water with an oar. But the mystery was answered as the captain of the surfmen rowed frantically to shore, shouting that he'd seen a shark. In an uproar, more than a hundred men, women, and children ran shrieking from the Asbury Avenue beach. It did not require much urging of the guards to clear the water of the bathers.

The captain of the surfmen tried to calm the panic, telling all who would listen that "had he been armed with an ax or harpoon he might have succeeded in killing or wounding the shark." But as soon as Everingham reported the news to his superiors, Asbury Park officials closed the beach and ordered bathers out of the water at the Seventh Avenue bathing grounds as well. The Fourth Avenue beach, enclosed by protective steel nets, remained open that afternoon, but many bathers chose to leave the water. They sat huddled on the sand, watching armed patrol boats move up and down the coast outside the netting.

The shark aroused in men old angers and new possibilities of blood lust. The mayor immediately ordered shark hooks fashioned for his boat and announced that from then on, he would be fishing for sharks to keep them away from the populace. Harold Phillips, a member of the Asbury Park Fishing Club, declared he would tow the carcasses of horses and cows to a remote area a quarter mile off Sandy Hook. The carcasses would attract "the greatest roundup of sharks ever seen," Phillips promised, and then the fellows from the Asbury Park Gun Club would train their rifles "for what would no doubt prove most exciting sport, shooting the big game of the seas."

But Asbury Park officials were not reassured by plans to eradicate all the man-eaters in the ocean. By the end of the day, they announced that both the Asbury Avenue and the Seventh Avenue beaches would remain closed because of the "shark menace" until they could be surrounded by the steel-wire nets.

Philadelphia Public Ledger,
July 9, 1916

Whether the shark that attacked Everingham was the great white that killed Bruder didn't seem to matter; fear was growing general on the coast at the pace that hysteria outruns reason. One shark now represented all sharks, white or blue, near or far from shore. Two days after the death of Charles Bruder in Spring Lake, declared the *Asbury Park Press*, "The shark scare in Asbury Park has become a reality."

The news of Bruder's death flew that summer from Manasquan to Massachusetts to Virginia and along five hundred miles of coastline. Whether borne by word of mouth or by printing press, the story traveled the shortest distance to the frightened heart, for it was the oldest suspense story of all—man killed by monster.

The very day Ben Everingham clubbed an attacking shark at Asbury Park, a score of boys and girls were bathing near the Robbins Reef Yacht Club in Bayonne, New Jersey, when several of the children saw something black, a shark, some eight feet long, appear off the float that extended out from the clubhouse.

Somebody yelled, "It's a shark!" and the children ran, screaming, for the bathhouses.

Police lieutenant Dennis Colohan was working nearby and had his revolver with him. He quickly ran to the end of the float. The shark was still coming, headed toward shore. Colohan waited until the big fish was twenty feet away. He saw that the fin alone was three feet high out of the water and he squeezed the trigger. Some of the shots lodged in the shark's head and yet the shark kept coming and Colohan kept shooting, emptying the revolver. The shark "seemed stunned for a moment, and then, lashing its tail, it turned quickly about, headed toward the Robbins Reef Lighthouse, and disappeared," Colohan said. The next day he was a hero, elevated by the *World* to the same pedestal as Everingham: "Two More Sharks Sighted and Sent to Sea a-Grieving."

More than two hundred miles south, along the coasts of Maryland and Virginia, swimmers and boaters saw the ocean and the waters of Chesapeake Bay as something menacing and foreign. *The Washington Star* urged swimmers to beware of whatever had killed two men in New Jersey. Hundreds of thousands of people on the Atlantic coast were now afraid to go in the water, the *Star* noted, for good reason.

A warning came from silent-film star and world-renowned beauty Annette Kellerman, who in 1914 starred in *Neptune's Daughter* and was then appearing as a mermaid in *A Daughter of the Gods*. "Whether . . . Bruder was killed by the dreaded shark or by some other species of large fish," Kellerman was moved to write in a major article in *The Washington Post*, "something in the water . . . attacked him and tore his limbs from the body, that we do know."

New York Herald,
July 9, 1916

The world's most famous female swimmer, Kellerman was an early prophet of swimming as a safe, democratic, and wholesome sport. Now, in July 1916, she urged Americans to accept a hidden danger inherent in swimming: to fear sharks and to raise their children to fear them, especially the white shark. Well known to Australians, the white was "the nearest to what we term man-eater," for it "will attack with terrific ferocity, and nothing will stop him from attaining his end." In Australia, "from the time a child is able to understand things the fear of the shark is forcibly impressed upon the mind. The shark to an Australian child occupies the same position as the bogeyman does to American children."

She closed her essay with a prescient warning: "That shark that killed Bruder will hover about the spot and perhaps others will join him. Then we will be subjected to a reign of terror that will cause the public to shun the beaches and bring ruin to the bathing-house owners."

That same morning in Spring Lake, the soul of Charles Bruder was committed to eternal life at a funeral service at St. Andrew's Methodist Church, as employees of the Essex and Sussex and other hotels filled the pews. Outside, patrol boats buzzed along the coast through a steaming summer morning, and rowboats packed with armed men moored near the north and south bathing pavilions. Despite the heat, the beaches were almost empty.

The next morning, Sunday, July 9, Asbury Park's summer people in the hotels and cottages strolled down the boulevards to the sea. Trolley car 32 was swollen with passengers bound for the beaches, for "visitors and hotel guests had fully regained their confidence," the *Asbury Park Press* reported.

The beaches were thronged with crowds, the water aswarm with bathers who appeared to have forgotten the deaths of Charles Vansant

The Washington Post, July 16, 1916

and Charles Bruder with the denial that attended shark attacks. For if nothing could be more horrible than being swallowed by a monster fish, what could be more rewarding than to forget?

Besides, sharks were nothing to worry about now. Only one day after hysteria swept Asbury Park, "the shark scare . . . is practically dead," the *Press* crowed, "albeit there are sharks somewhere in the ocean and whales, too, for that matter. But Asbury Park's bathing grounds are free from sharks for the very simple reason that no sharks can enter them." The beaches were all barricaded by steel wire that formed a U shape around the bathing grounds. Even in Spring Lake, three days after Bruder's death, beach attendance was improving. While bathers were "loath to venture very far out," the *Press* reported, "it is possible early next week will again see bathing in vogue."

Bathers were reassured by the comments that week by Hugh Smith, director of the U.S. Bureau of Fisheries, that they ought "not be unduly alarmed or deterred from going in bathing," as "sharks are not vicious." Like Dr. Lucas, Hugh Smith had studied sharks for years and shared his opinion that a shark had not killed Bruder or Vansant.

The commissioner believed the likeliest culprit in both men's deaths was the broadbill swordfish, *Xiphias gladius,* whose tall dorsal fin would explain the fins sighted during both attacks. The swordfish possesses great speed and enormous size—up to fifteen feet long and a thousand pounds—and there were reports, the commissioner said, of men run cleanly through by its long, flat sword.

"When we consider that there are hundreds of thousands of bathers on our eastern coasts every year and that for as long as anyone can remember no one has been bitten until these two recent cases, I think it is a word in favor of the sharks," Smith said. "Our domestic animals, horses, dogs, and others, have not anything like this record."

HUNGER OR MADNESS

As the sun slid into the sea along the darkening coast, the shark descended with it, plunging thirty, forty feet to the bottom, where it cruised on the pebbly landscape of the ocean floor. Schools of big blackfish and hordes of cunners moved in and out of the wrecks maddeningly, somehow beyond reach.

It was unable to feed as it was accustomed. The fish of the mid-Atlantic were well organized in classes of predator and prey, a natural structure from which the shark had somehow removed itself or been removed through illness or failure. In the brute and unsparing choreography of nature, it no longer held a proper part.

On the coast of southern and central New Jersey, old-time fishermen were now speculating that the man-eater, whatever it was, would drift north in coastal currents—and this conclusion would prove to be right. The pounding blows of an oar off Asbury Park, the gunshots splitting the waves of Spring Lake, were like larger predators frightening it north with the currents into a world that no longer sustained it. Its hunger or its madness was reaching an urgent point.

Yet the shark was adapted to handle the crisis of hunger in ways human beings did not know in 1916, and struggled decades later to understand. As the shark swam, there is evidence the legs and bones of Charles Bruder cut off at the knees and pieces of the bell captain's torso remained preserved in the fish's stomach for later consumption, in the manner of a camel. Gleaming specimens of dolphins and mackerel, fresh as if iced in the fishmonger's window, have been pulled from the stomachs of sharks, as well as still-legible paper documents. But the most compelling proof of the shark's camel-like ability in crisis occurred on April 17, 1935, when Albert Hobston caught a thirteen-foot tiger shark off a Sydney, Australia, beach and towed it alive to the Coogee Aquarium. Eight days later, dying in captivity, the shark regurgitated a bird, a rat, and, eerily visible in a cloud of muck, a human arm—a thick, muscular arm, so well preserved that the forearm was clearly marked with a tattoo of two boxers. On the basis of a photograph of the tattoo, published in a Sydney newspaper, a man identified his brother, James Smith. The arm was preserved so well, it was accepted as evidence that led to the arrest of a man for murdering and dismembering Smith and dumping him at sea.

In the cooler coastal waters that week, the great white's body temperature lowered and its rate of digestion slowed. Gradually, the shark digested the flesh from a pair of human legs, gaining nutrition. The bones were indigestible, and the shark would later expel them with turtle shells and porpoise bones—like a dog retching up chicken bones. But Charles Bruder's remains wouldn't sustain the shark for long. It may be difficult to understand that a young great white shark could falter in its native environment, that in the ocean wild animals make mistakes unprovoked by man, get themselves into situations they cannot get out of.

Lost, hungry, the ocean's foremost predator was still formidable. At nearly eight feet and four hundred pounds, it was a seed of what it would become. How large white sharks grow is unknown, but the largest documented was almost twenty feet and several tons. The young shark would simply grow as long as it lived, and no human knew what gigantism it could attain. Its life would be lengthy, half a century or more, and remarkably hardy. It would be free of cancer, infections, circulatory diseases, competition. Its wounds would heal themselves with a speed people associate with science fiction. But there were limits to the great white's power, and in July 1916, the young white moved like a creature raging against those limits.

After days of swimming north along the shore, it came to the northernmost tip of the Jersey coast, the Sandy Hook peninsula. To the east was the open ocean, but following its instinct to hug the coast, the shark cruised around the tip of Sandy Hook and left the ocean for good, curling into Sandy Hook Bay. From the deep, clean currents of the Atlantic, the big fish now wallowed in five and six and eight feet of bay water.

Of the more than four hundred species of sharks, only a few can pass from salt to fresh water. The great white could survive in brackish water, but only temporarily. In brackish water, a great white loses the salt balance between its body and the water. To restore the equilibrium, the shark's flesh loses salt to the water, and slowly its basic physiological functions shut down. For a short time only, the shark's huge mass would protect it from feeling the deadly effects.

The young white meandered west, winding around the mouths of creeks and rivers and harbors, hugging the shore, traveling farther from the life-giving sea. Familiar prey was gone, and the shark became further weakened. Sluggishness heightened its urgency to feed. Confusion or sluggishness was certain death.

The mouth of Matawan Creek is wide enough for a fish to mistake it for the shoreline, and so on that morning, the great white shark hewed to the coast and turned into the creek, surely unaware it had left Raritan Bay. The shark swept into the creek on the high tide, surging in on currents of salt water. Yet not far from the mouth of the creek, the inland waterway dramatically narrows, tapering down from two hundred feet across to a hundred to fifty to barely twenty. Within a few sweeps of its powerful tail the shark entered a diminishing world, murky and sluicing with fresh water, and it grew unsettled.

This was a situation it had never encountered before. The world it was born into had no walls or edges. The sea was forever. There were only two boundaries: the beach and the bottom. In brackish water, with the bottom and sides closing in, the shark may have experienced a kind of claustrophobia, shark biologists speculate. By the time the shark became aware of its mistake, it found it difficult to escape the small waterway. Perhaps it tried and failed to return to the sea, redoubling its frustration. In alien environments, sharks become weakened, desperate, highly agitated.

Yet as it swam with slackening thrusts of its tail, the shark detected signals that washed about its lateral line through the brown and clouded water, signals of interest, thrumming with sonic and then olfactory cues and then explosions, signals of prey. A mile and a half ahead, as the creek wended in a lazy S shape through the sedge marshes, lay the town of Matawan.

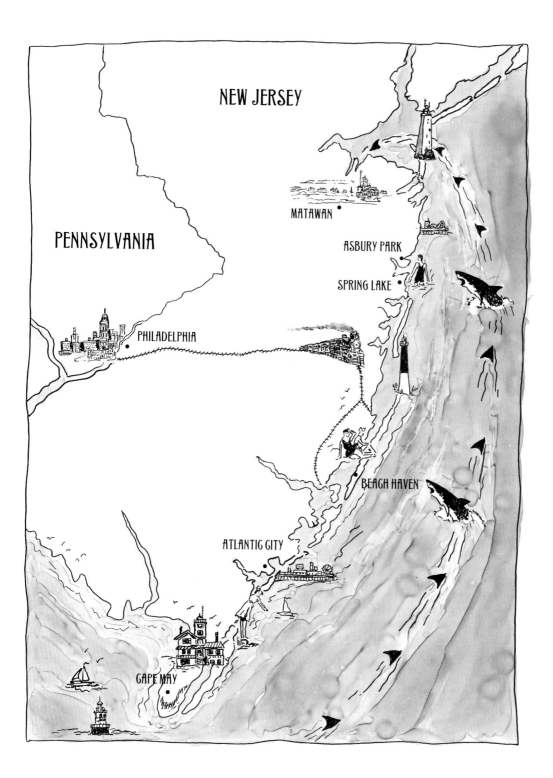

NEW JERSEY

PENNSYLVANIA

MATAWAN

ASBURY PARK

SPRING LAKE

PHILADELPHIA

BEACH HAVEN

ATLANTIC CITY

CAPE MAY

THE GREEK

 Seventeen miles inland from Asbury Park, on the banks of Matawan Creek, was a typical early-twentieth-century American small town. Main Street rolled through its center, paralleling the creek, where flat-bottom boats set out with loads of tomatoes from the farm country. The tallest structures were the white church spires, which rose up over the shops and the fine houses that marched down the length of Main under elms and sycamores.

More of the outside world was coming and going through towns in the new century, but little of it stayed or altered the people of Matawan. If any change was most profound, it was that the goods and people and ideas now came by locomotive and motorcar and wire; the town had stopped producing generations of rugged sea captains and fishermen. It was losing its old link to the sea.

Many of the citizens of Matawan considered themselves modern and sophisticated, for they had time—freed at last from plowing and planting—for leisure. The domino tournament was the talk of the town. On the Fourth of July, men played the ladies' baseball team wearing long Victorian dresses—all except the mayor, who dressed like Uncle Sam.

Yet the industries that gave men and women the money and time for leisure in Matawan—the town made tiles, matches, candy, pianos, baskets and bottles, waxes, asphalt, and copper castings—crowded portions of the creek and the land beyond with factories and tainted the air. By 1916, the creek was dotted here and there with manufacturers but still wound

A boathouse on Matawan
Creek, circa 1915

through vast, tranquil prairies of *Spartina* grass and sky. And so Matawan Creek flowed as an increasingly sentimental link to the rural and romantic past. The creek was the beloved heart of the town.

The afternoon of July 11, a hot summer day, Rensselaer "Renny" Cartan Jr. left the Cartan Lumber and Coal Company, his father's business, and walked down the street to find his cousin, Johnson Cartan. Johnson stocked shelves at Cartan's Department Store. Renny and Johnson cut down a bank to the creek, winding through tall grasses toward the swimming hole. Skinny-dipping in the old swimming hole was a Matawan tradition going back generations, and all the businessmen along Main let their sons and hired boys go to cool off for a few minutes every afternoon.

The boys scrambled onto the pier and pilings and threw off their clothes, laughing and shouting. Renny Cartan was standing naked on a dock piling, joking with his cousin and friends, when he began to lose his balance. The creek was only thirty feet wide and shallow, but the water was darker than usual with the turbulence of recent rains and Renny couldn't see the bottom, couldn't see what he'd be hitting as he fell. But Renny Cartan gave in to gravity and the joy of the moment and let himself go, laughing, into the creek. The other boys leapt into the creek as well, their legs disappearing in darkness toward the bottom, mucky and cool between their toes.

Moments after Rensselaer Cartan entered the water of Matawan Creek, it betrayed him. A refreshing dip gave way to a searing warmth ripping across his chest. It was a strange sensation that fourteen years of experience couldn't process. He was bleeding and he didn't know what was in the water.

The splashing in the swimming hole, barely a mile from the mouth of the creek, had drawn the great white shark to investigate. The creek teemed with life, but none of it large enough to sustain a great white shark. So when the shark spied the whirling porcelain limbs of the boy underwater, it grew excited and charged. In the view of some researchers, the shark's pass may have been investigative or even a form of play. There are numerous accounts of sharks bumping surfboards and surfers and not attacking, frolicking in a rather one-sided game only the apex predator understands. But the great white's true motive that afternoon was likely ominous. Shark attacks on man are often preceded by a bump that causes gashing wounds. The purpose of the bump seems to be to determine the size and strength of possible prey.

Renny Cartan had no idea he had been bumped and scraped by a great white shark. He knew only that it didn't hurt at first, then the pain was like hot needles, and larger than the pain was the loss of control and the unknowing. In that instant he saw something dark moving in the water, something larger than any fish he had ever seen. And then it was gone.

Renny Cartan scrambled out of the creek, screaming. His chest was bloodied, as if raked by the tips of knives. The other boys, streaked with mud, crowded around, trying to calm him. Cartan would not be calmed. He said he had been hit and wounded by something in the creek, something huge. None of the other boys had seen it. Renny's wounds looked painful but not serious, as though he had scratched himself on a branch. His friends listened as long as boys do when play has been interrupted and awaits and is calling them back. Soon Renny's cousin Johnson and the other boys scurried onto the dock and leapt back into the creek.

As Renny Cartan left the creek to get his wounds bandaged, he shouted at his friends to get out of the water, but his warning fell on deaf ears. After Renny left the swimming hole, his friends shouted and splashed and jumped from the dock, unaware that sonic cues were now exploding along the narrow banks of the creek to a great white shark, a shark that had taken the measure of the noisy mammals and was slashing through the brackish water, highly stimulated.

The next morning, Wednesday, July 12, Thomas V. Cottrell, a retired sea captain, set out from his house at the mouth of the creek for his customary walk. The old captain was an incorrigible storyteller and jokester, a man of a hundred friends and a thousand tales.

As the captain strolled along the creek that morning, he found himself staring at the brown water more intently than usual. The captain had heard of the boy who cried wolf the day before, about something in the creek that bit or scratched him, and he felt bad for the boy, and a bit curious over what manner of fish Renny Cartan had seen. Then, walking over the new trolley bridge spanning Matawan Creek, he saw something for which neither man nor God, tide nor typhoon, had prepared him.

Rippling up the muddy waters of the creek, toward the bridge, was a large dark-gray shape trailing a long, pointed dorsal fin. In the moment it took for shock and disbelief to subside, Captain Cottrell recognized it as a shark, a big one, winding slowly up the tidal creek. As the shark swam closer to him, it loomed bigger still, a wide, gray-brown fish, possibly nine or ten feet long, until it passed directly under Cottrell and slipped under the bridge. He turned to watch the fin disappearing up the creek. Thomas Cottrell realized with an incredulous shudder that the shark was headed unswervingly toward town.

The captain was on the move as well. The town of Matawan could not have placed a better sentinel for the approach of the shark than Thomas V. Cottrell. The captain had brine in his veins and was accustomed to thinking under pressure. He had taken note of the newspaper stories about two recent shark deaths on the Jersey coast and wondered if it was the same shark. Captain Cottrell was of the lot of seafarers who took shark legends seriously. And so, pumping new life into his aging seaman's legs, Cottrell turned around on the bridge and raced toward town, hoping to reach town before the shark.

When Thomas Cottrell pushed open the door of John Mulsoff's barbershop, the men gathered there fell silent, for the old sea captain was gasping for breath, his face animated with a crazed look. Mulsoff, the barber who moonlighted as the town constable, was one of the most admired men in town. But the old sea captain's story about a shark from the ocean, headed up the creek toward town, sounded mad. John Mulsoff considered it for a moment, tipped back his head, and laughed incredulously. Disbelieving chuckles rounded the barbershop. Flushed with anger and embarrassment, Cottrell stumbled out of the shop and took his story urgently to the sidewalk, where a cluster of merchants met him with more skepticism and puzzled looks. A shark in the creek? Old Cottrell must have been in one too many nor'easters. With growing frustration, the sea captain pressed his case up and down Main Street, to men who'd known him for years and admired his sea stories, but "everywhere the captain was laughed at," *The New York Times* reported. "How could a shark get ten miles away from the ocean, swim through Raritan Bay, and enter the shallow creek with only seventeen feet of water at its deepest spot and nowhere more than thirty-five feet wide? So grown-ups and children flocked to the creek as usual for their daily dip."

Thomas Cottrell had not survived forty years at sea by distrusting his own instincts. He hurried down to the docks by the creek and climbed in his small motorboat, the *Skud*. Coaxing the motorboat to a hiccuping start, he gave it some gas. He was soon chugging up the creek, cruising the center channel, on the water, where he'd felt in command all his life, but perhaps never so out of control as now. Shielding the sun with his hand, he scanned the narrowing distance for a fin and the boyish heads of swimmers. As he motored, he shouted warnings of a shark, shouted out over the creek until he was hoarse.

A great dorsal fin sliced the middle of the brown creek as the shark swam along deserted banks, undetected by anyone.

Also unseen, in the bright afternoon sky, the moon's orbit was on a course that would put it in the earth's shadow two days later. The coming lunar eclipse of July 14, 1916, held no interest for scientists then, but the phases of the moon were fundamental to the shark. The hidden moon was waxing, three days from full, radiating near-maximum gravitational pull, and the great white was growing excited and vibrant in reaction to the moon's surging power. Around the world, ocean tides were rising, and the tide was coming up Matawan Creek now, swelling the banks and lifting the shark, bracing it with life-giving seawater.

The shark was moving upriver no faster than a walking man, swaying its body from side to side, smelling the water and processing information with great rapidity.

The citizens of Matawan in 1916 would not have laughed at the idea that the full moon exerted a powerful effect on people, plants, and animals. It was well known at the time that "lunacy" gripped the residents of jails and mental hospitals during the full moon. Evil preyed on human beings under a full moon. If by 1916 lunar superstitions were the fodder of emerging modern entertainment (*Dracula* was a popular novel), other myths continued to flourish. Moonlight is harmful to the health, the not-yet-old wives' tales said; fleece will be lighter if sheared when the moon is waning; wood cut in the waxing of the moon will be "sappy"; fish will bite more on the night of a full moon.

Later, scientists would find evidence that sharks attack more frequently during very high tides, caused by the gravitational pull of the full moon. A preliminary study by researchers for the International Shark Attack File has found a worldwide correlation between "the phases of the moon, the height of tides and the frequency of shark attacks." Researchers are studying the phenomenon, and while there is yet no conclusive proof the white shark fits the pattern, "a study of white sharks near South Africa shows a peak in attacks at the highest of high tides."

There are several possible explanations for lunar-related shark attacks. Sharks could be reacting to the effect of the moon on other ocean species. The reproduction of many types of fish coincides with the cycles of the moon. High tides also reduce beach space, drawing prey such as seals into the water and sharks nearer shore.

Whatever the reason, as the juvenile great white shark cruised through the murky waters of Matawan Creek, the moon would soon be at its most luminous, the creek tides rising to the highest recorded levels of the month.

AN UNEVEN BATTLE

In the low gloom of a factory, the hammer blurred as if trailing sparks, and in less than a minute the battered hands of William Stilwell held a delicate but sturdy round basket. Swiftly, Stilwell struck another basket into existence and stacked it with the others. The shouts of the line boss and the thudding of hammers wielded by men and boys along the bench filled the scorching, humid air. But the line boss paid fifty cents for a hundred baskets, and Stilwell worked with the speed of a man who had five young children to feed and could take home three dollars that day if he raced.

As the sun slanted over the creek and Bill Stilwell had passed a couple of hundred baskets, he saw the line boss give a nod, and the younger boys dropped their hammers and made for the door, Stilwell's youngest son, Lester, with them. It was a tradition for the boys to sneak away to the creek on summer days. Lester dutifully ran up to his father to say good-bye, and Bill told him to be careful and stay near the dock.

Shortly before two o'clock, Lester Stilwell was running free on Main Street. He met up with friends, moving quickly since their fathers and bosses cut them only a few minutes, and the six boys went down to Dock Road, cutting behind the barn to the creek. The boys threw their clothes on the banks and began diving off the dilapidated docks at the old steamboat landing. One by one, they dove and stroked to the middle of the creek, then swam back to the docks and dove again.

Lester Stilwell cried, "Watch me float, fellas!" and in the next instant, Charlie Van Brunt saw what he called "the biggest, blackest fish he had ever seen" streaking underwater for Lester. Charlie saw the shark strike, twisting and rolling as it hit Lester, exhibiting its stark white belly and gleaming teeth. As the boys looked on in horror, they saw Lester's arm in the mouth of the shark and "Lester, being shaken, like a cat shakes a mouse, and then he went under, head first." As the shark jerked the boy underwater, it gave such a mighty swish through the water that its tail hit Albert O'Hara and knocked him against the pilings supporting the pier. For a horrific second, Lester Stilwell reappeared, rising out of the water screaming and waving his arms wildly. Then, in an instant, he was pulled back under and disappeared for good.

Small waves had upset the waters of the creek, but they were smoothing and the water was crimson where Lester had been. Suddenly boys cried, "Oh my God, he's gone!" and swam and stumbled and scrambled out of the water and up on the muddy banks, crying, "Shark! Shark!" Rushing in a group past their heaped clothes, the five boys ran naked down Dock Road and turned right on Main. Frank Clowes was leading them, for he was the oldest, but they were all running dripping wet and wild-eyed into the heart of town.

The children hollered, "Shark! A shark got Lester!" to anyone who would listen. A crowd surrounded the boys, trying to calm them. Constable Mulsoff, hurrying to the commotion from the barbershop, had a crisis on his hands. Mulsoff thought it eerie that young Stilwell had disappeared shortly after Captain Cottrell's crazed warning of a shark, but the constable was a sturdy and rational man and the boys' claims were scarcely more believable than the captain's. Moving quickly, the constable rounded up a group of men and marched them toward the creek to rescue the boy, or, more likely, to recover his drowned body.

Upset that no one believed their story of a shark, some of the boys continued on down Main to the door of the Royal Tailors, where Stanley Fisher was sewing a custom suit. Some town residents "thought the boys were playing a prank until finally they appealed to Stanley Fisher," the *New York Herald* reported. "They knew he was a powerful swimmer . . . and a friend of all the boys in town."

Fisher promptly closed the shop. But not before he slipped into the back room and put on a bathing costume. Out on Main Street, the big tailor ran into his childhood friend George Burlew. Burlew's dream was to be a big-game fisherman, and the idea of a shark excited him, although he, too, assumed it couldn't be true.

A huge crowd of townspeople was already gathered along the dock and banks of Matawan Creek. Men in rowboats soberly patrolled the banks, poling the murky water. Bill and Luella Stilwell and their other son and daughters stared in shock at the spot where Lester had vanished. The arrival of Stanley Fisher sent a wave of anticipation through the crowd.

Fisher quickly took command. He and Burlew climbed into a rowboat and strung chicken wire weighted with stones in the shallower water downcreek, stretching a barrier twenty feet from bank to bank, "so the tide wouldn't take the body out," Burlew recalled. Fisher and Burlew joined the others poling for the body, but after an hour with no success, Fisher and Burlew dove overboard.

Shouts and warnings to watch out for a shark sounded from the banks, but the men ignored them and swam to the middle of the creek, where they began to make dives to the deep center channel, where the poling couldn't reach and where Fisher believed Stilwell's body had sunk. The men plunged toward the creek bottom, disappearing for several moments, then surfacing, gasping for air. The creek was so murky, Fisher and Burlew said they couldn't see anything, and the bottom of the channel was too deep to reach. After almost half an hour of exhausting dives, they paused to discuss what to do. They concluded there was nothing more they *could* do except perhaps wait for low tide to reveal Lester Stilwell's body. Fisher and Burlew swam slowly back toward the bank.

Fisher abruptly decided to make one more dive for the bottom, and, upending his big body, plunged under the surface. But again he came up empty-handed. Ignoring pleas to call off the search, Fisher plunged once more toward the bottom. George Burlew was nearing the dock when he heard his friend break the surface and cry, "I've got it!" Shouts and cheers ringed the shore. Fisher had found Lester Stilwell! George swam out to help his friend, but the sensation of the water churning furiously caused him to stop.

Stanley Fisher now called, "He's got me!" Screaming and fighting for his life, Fisher was caught in the jaws of a shark. Years later, when George Burlew became a world-renowned big-game fisherman, he was better able to evaluate what he witnessed. "I never saw the entire fish," he recalled, "but from the tremendous upheaval of the huge tail that thrashed above the water it had to be a big one."

Stanley Fisher, circa 1916

Burlew was astonished at Fisher's courage. "Stanley was a big man, and he fought back at the shark, striking it with his fists," Burlew recalled. "He was fighting desperately to break away, striking and kicking at it with all his might. He seemed to be holding his own, but at best it was an uneven battle. The shark was at home in the water—and Stanley wasn't."

Fisher managed to get his head once again above water, but suddenly "he was jerked under again and the men in the boat saw the dirty white belly of the shark as he turned and went down. Then the water became crimson in a constantly widening area, and when Fisher came up next he was so exhausted he could hardly call out."

Men and women stood frozen on the banks, and George Burlew, too, found himself unable to move to help his friend. Battling the big fish alone, Fisher, incredibly, had fought himself free of the shark. With astonishing purpose, he swam toward the bank. The shocked crowd saw that Fisher had one arm around Lester Stilwell, or what remained of the boy. Three of Fisher's friends tried to rescue him, but their motorboat stalled in the creek and the men frantically paddled with their hands to reach Fisher. Other boatmen managed to row close to try to provide cover for him, slapping the water with oars to keep away the shark.

Fisher had nearly reached the bank of the creek when witnesses heard him utter a terrible cry and saw him throw his arms in the air. Stilwell's body fell into the creek, and with another desperate shout Fisher was dragged in after it, disappearing completely underwater.

"The shark! The shark!" people screamed. But Fisher, with remarkable fortitude, struggled once again toward the bank. Stilwell's body had disappeared; the shark had apparently fled with it. Fisher was able to keep his head above water now, but as the rescuers reached him, the men in the boat saw that most of the flesh between the hip and the knee of the right leg had been taken off.

Not until Stanley Fisher attempted to climb up the bank of the creek did he realize what had happened. He lifted his leg to examine it, said, "Oh, my God," and dropped back into the water again. Several men hauled Fisher onto the bank, where he lay in a rapidly spreading pool of his own blood. A rope was wrapped around the damaged leg near the hip, forming a tourniquet, and calls for a doctor resounded.

Men and women ran from the docks up to town and to Doc

Jackson's, but the doctor was out of town. Dr. George L. Reynolds was also not at home. Next on the list was Dr. Straughn. But Dr. Straughn had left the day before for a physicians' meeting. With the makeshift tourniquet on his leg, Fisher lay by the creek for half an hour until Dr. Reynolds was finally located and brought to the scene.

Reynolds had never seen such an injury. A wide, open wound, it stretched eighteen inches from below Fisher's hip to just above his knee. At the edges the flesh was ragged, as if fistfuls of flesh had been extracted, Reynolds observed, by a set of "dull knives." The femur, while scratched, was not penetrated. But the femoral artery, bleeding profusely, was completely severed. Despite the severity of the wounds, Stanley Fisher was still conscious, and as Dr. Reynolds worked to bind the huge bite, Fisher described how he had seen the shark feeding on Lester Stilwell's body and how, when he tried to recover the boy's body, the shark had released it and attacked him.

The wound bound as well as possible, Dr. Reynolds ordered men to build a stretcher. Working quickly, they cobbled together wooden planks, and a group of them strained to lift the 210-pound Fisher and bear him to the Matawan train station. The nearest hospital was ten miles east in Long Branch, and apparently the doctor didn't believe Fisher would survive the trip in an automobile. The next train to Long Branch left Matawan at 5:06 P.M. and would arrive at 7:45 P.M. Fisher had suffered what specialists would describe as a grade two shark attack—dire injuries that could be survived with prompt emergency treatment. That afternoon in 1916, however, the treatment Stanley Fisher required was two hours and thirty-nine minutes away.

"I THOUGHT IT WAS GOING TO SWALLOW ME"

Farther downcreek toward the bay, Joseph Dunn, his brother Michael, and their friend Jerry Hollohan cut a trail through the brickyards to a dock over the creek. Joseph and Michael were spending the summer at Cliffwood, a quarter of a mile below Matawan. The creek tantalized boys with the legends of pirates and buried treasure. It was said Captain Kidd sailed on Raritan Bay and Blackbeard had come up the creek and attacked farmers and villagers.

That Wednesday afternoon, however, the boys were simply looking to cool off with a swim, and Joseph Dunn, the youngest, raced to get in the water first. The boys did not know that Lester Stilwell and Stanley Fisher had been attacked half an hour earlier, three-quarters of a mile away. Had Joseph looked upcreek, he might have seen a large fin trailing toward the brick docks; "the shark, after feasting on the Stilwell boy and . . . Fisher's flesh, was on his way out to sea again and still was hungry," the *New York Herald* wrote. "Apparently the shark had finished his disturbed meal in the channel at Matawan and, knowing as such creatures do that the tide was running out, had started back for the deeper water of the bay."

A quarter mile away, the small engine of the *Skud* beat the water as Captain Cottrell motored along bends in the creek, shouting his warnings to people on the banks and to any swimmers he could find. But the creek was wild and deserted for long stretches; the work was slow. After the attack on Lester Stilwell, a small armada had joined Cottrell. By the time Stanley Fisher was attacked, half a dozen motorboats were out on Matawan Creek, searching for the shark and spreading the warning.

"It would seem that few could miss such a warning," the *New York Herald* later reported. But Joseph Dunn and his companions were among the few. Dunn looked at the brown surface of the water and saw nothing but his own reflection. And so, at about four o'clock that afternoon, he jumped.

Dunn swam toward the middle of the creek. His brother Michael was in next, and then Jerry. Moments later, the warning finally reached the boys. A man ran to the creek, warning of a shark, and the boys swam quickly back toward the docks. Hollohan and Michael Dunn climbed the ladder out of the water and Joseph was swimming toward the ladder as fast as he could when something enormous and "very rough" struck him and scratched his skin.

"I was about ten feet from shore and looked down and saw something dark. . . . I did not see him the first time he hit me . . . then suddenly I felt a tug, like a big pair of scissors pulling at my leg and bringing me under. . . . I thought it was off. I felt as if my leg had gone." In fact, the shark's serrated teeth were grating and shredding Dunn's leg as it tried to pull the boy into deeper water, where it could attack and feed without distraction. Incredibly, Dunn felt very little pain. The screams came instead from a terrifying thought: "It seemed the fish was [trying] . . . to get my whole leg inside his mouth . . . I thought it was going to swallow me."

A shark attack on a human being evolves from an unlikely sequence of rare events, and rescue attempts, too, are governed by chains of extraordinary occurrences. So it was that Jacob Lefferts was motoring downcreek in his boat, issuing shark warnings, when he witnessed the Dunn attack. And not far behind him, in the *Skud*, came Captain Cottrell.

Lefferts, fully clothed, dove into the creek toward the attacking shark, while at the same time Michael Dunn swam to his brother's aid. Man and boy grabbed Joseph Dunn and attempted to wrestle him from the mouth of the shark. Somehow Joseph and his rescuers made it as far as the dock ladder. "As he drew himself up on the brick company's pier, with only his left leg trailing in the water, the shark struck at that," *The New York Times* reported. "Its teeth shut over the leg above and below the knee and much of the flesh was torn away."

At last the shark let go of Dunn, and his companions dragged him, yelling, up onto the pier. The boy's wounds appeared ghastly. After hasty attempts to stop the bleeding with makeshift bandages, Lefferts, Captain Cottrell, and Michael Dunn lowered the stricken boy into Cottrell's motorboat.

As the *Skud* led the rescue party upcreek, Captain Cottrell noticed how far the tide had gone out. It was only the shallowness of the creek at the brickyard docks, he thought, that had prevented the shark from swiftly making off with Joseph Dunn in its jaws. It had been pure luck that he had reached the boy in time. In the old days, when the big boats went all the way up to Matawan, before the creek silted in, the shark would have had a deep and clear path to the bay. Racing back along the S curves of the creek, looking down at the small boy in his boat, Thomas Cottrell wondered if luck would matter.

The shark had vanished from human view, camouflaged by the dark creek water, leaving no trace of its presence but the distant shouts of men and a small wake washing diluted blood to the banks. Releasing huge stores of energy summoned during its attacking frenzy, the shark was fleeing for safety. It did not know fear but responded to danger, and certainly there was threat from the men and boats on the creek.

The attacks on Stanley Fisher and Lester Stilwell had not sated the shark for long; more than ten pounds of human flesh was a small meal. The shark's life consisted of taking ten, twenty, forty pounds of fish in a single meal and moving ever onward for more. All that had changed was that the meals now included humans. The brackish water weakened the shark, and the confines of the creek were disorienting. So the big fish hurtled down-creek, seeking a return to that open world, the world of the sea.

Yet everywhere it traveled in this small space, driven by hunger, it sensed the lure of prey. Far ahead in the creek, pulses exploded underwater, sounds and scents that shortened the closing distance. Above in the deep-ening sky the moon was waxing, intensifying its brightness and its pull on tides and fish and the predatory instincts of sharks. The shark made a series of adjustments in the set of its pectoral fins and the thrust of its tail, hunt-ing now in a frenetic state.

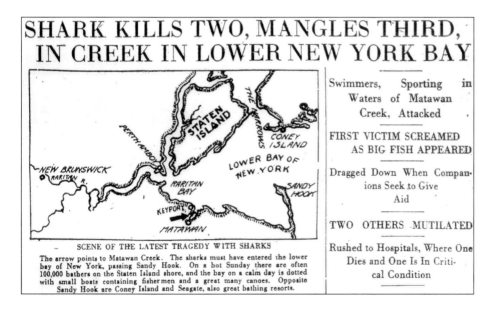

SHARK KILLS TWO, MANGLES THIRD, IN CREEK IN LOWER NEW YORK BAY

SCENE OF THE LATEST TRAGEDY WITH SHARKS

The arrow points to Matawan Creek. The sharks must have entered the lower bay of New York, passing Sandy Hook. On a hot Sunday there are often 100,000 bathers on the Staten Island shore, and the bay on a calm day is dotted with small boats containing fishermen and a great many canoes. Opposite Sandy Hook are Coney Island and Seagate, also great bathing resorts.

Swimmers, Sporting in Waters of Matawan Creek, Attacked

FIRST VICTIM SCREAMED AS BIG FISH APPEARED

Dragged Down When Companions Seek to Give Aid

TWO OTHERS MUTILATED

Rushed to Hospitals, Where One Dies and One Is In Critical Condition

Philadelphia Public Ledger,
July 13, 1916

TO SEE ITS BODY DRAWN UP ON THE SHORE

Down Main Street, in house after house, and in the farmhouses on the outskirts of town, men reached above the fireplace and in the corner of the barn for shotgun, rifle, and harpoon. The word at the creek was that the shark was trapped. Wire nets had been stretched across the creek near Keyport, where it emptied into the bay, to block the shark's escape. When A. B. Henderson, the acting mayor of Matawan, announced the borough would pay a one-hundred-dollar bounty "to the person who killed the shark," an emotional torrent swept along the banks.

WHERE A SHARK KILLED A MAN AND A BOY IN MATAWAN CREEK

Photograph by International Film Service

Hundreds joined in the hunt on Wednesday afternoon and all night long for the man-eater and one of its victims. In boats and on the banks of the stream they were equally unsuccessful

Philadelphia Public Ledger,
July 14, 1916

As five o'clock approached, the constable gave a signal to clear the creek of boats. Men with rifles and jittery trigger fingers scanned the surface of the creek for movement. The slightest quivers of fish aroused shouts of "There! There!" But the gunmen were ordered to hold their fire while others on the banks carefully prepared explosives. The citizens of Matawan knew nothing of the shark's weaknesses or habits, only that it was a man-eater. And that the destroyer could be met only by destruction.

Watching from the banks, Bill and Luella Stilwell prayed that if Lester was now dead, at least his body could be recovered for a proper Christian burial. But the unstated fear of the shark hunters was that the boy had been totally devoured by the shark. The men were convinced that dynamite offered the hope of killing the shark and of finding Lester's remains, if any. Fishermen had advised that "the shock of the explosions will stun the shark or burst the gall inside its body and cause it to rise to the surface." They did not know that the great white shark possesses no such flotation gall. Heavier than water, it must keep swimming or succumb to gravity. Unlike whales and other fish, it sinks when it dies.

Philadelphia Public Ledger,
July 14, 1916

Just before the first charge was to be set off, a motorboat appeared downcreek. Captain Cottrell stood at the wheel of the *Skud,* and as the boat drew nearer, Jacob Lefferts announced, "A shark got him!" Lying on the bottom of the boat was Joseph Dunn, his leg encased in bloodied bandages. The men laid down their guns and went to carry the boy—a boy Lester Stilwell's age—onto the dock.

Dr. Herbert Cooley of Keyport had responded too late to the summons to help Lester Stilwell and Stanley Fisher, never suspecting yet another person would need emergency care for a shark attack within the hour. Like Dr. Reynolds, Dr. Cooley was reluctant to touch the ragged cut, fearing that sharks infected their victims with poisons. But the doctor persevered and

Brave Victim of Shark

Photograph by International Film Service
STANLEY FISHER
He went to the rescue of a boy in Matawan Creek and was so mangled that he died shortly after reaching a hospital

cleansed the wound as the half-conscious boy cried out. "The calf muscle was severely lacerated," the doctor later reported, "and the front and side of the boy's lower left leg were cut into ribbons from knee to the ankle." If there was good news, it was that "the bones were not crushed and the main arteries in the calf of the leg were not cut." From the perspective of half a century later, Dunn had suffered grade three shark wounds, the most common and most minor arterial, abdominal, or limb damage. In such cases the victim is expected to survive if treated immediately.

Having wrapped the wound with clean bandages, Dr. Cooley instructed a bystander to rush the boy and him to the hospital, assuming he was treating a mortal injury. As the roadster throttled north, Dr. Cooley fought the certainty that the boy would soon die, overcome by toxins from a poisoned bite.

In the villages of Matawan and Keyport, whistles ended the day in the plants that had not already emptied, and more men with guns as well as curious women and children streamed down through the grasses to the creek to join the mob. Now the waterway once again was cleared of boats. At Constable Mulsoff's signal, a dynamite blast sent a geyser of muddy water high over the crowd.

At 5:06 that afternoon, Fisher, fully conscious after more than an hour's wait, had been carried aboard the train bound for Long Beach. Some two and a half hours later, Fisher reached the operating table at Monmouth Memorial, where, still conscious, he told his surgeons he had wrested Stilwell's corpse from the shark's mouth. After five minutes on the operating table, Stanley Fisher died from massive blood loss and hemorrhagic shock.

Shark Kills Man in Battle for Body of Boy; Cripples Another Lad Off Raritan Shore

After eight o'clock, when darkness had settled on the creek, word reached the banks that Fisher was dead, and feelings of powerlessness and dread swept through the growing crowd. "Tonight the whole town is stirred by a personal feeling," *The New York Times* reported, "a feeling which makes men regard the fish as they might a human being who had taken the lives of a boy and a youth and badly, perhaps mortally, injured another youngster."

With no understanding of the shark, there was no place to put fear except into rage. Crowded along the banks, men lifted rifles and bullets ripped into the water. Onlookers scurried for cover from dynamite blasts and the tranquil creek erupted as if a primal force had been loosed. Small fish eviscerated by the blasts floated on the surface. Between dynamite blasts, men trolled the dark creek in boats, working in eerie ribbons of lantern light, dredging the creek bottom with oyster hoops. During cease-fires, more than a hundred armed men in boats patrolled up and down the creek, scanning for ripples that signaled the man-eater. Reporters crowded closer to the townsfolk on the banks with their notebooks and visions of a village besieged by a sea monster. Despite the bright light of the moon, there were no sharks in sight, but that hardly mattered as men shot and bombed everything that stirred. "The one purpose in which everybody shares," the *Times* reported, "is to get the shark, to kill it, and to see its body drawn up on the shore, where all may look and be assured it will destroy no more."

The Jersey roads were gravel and the roadster wheezed and shimmied as John Nichols crawled along at a frustrating pace. He had sped through New York at thirty miles an hour but couldn't exceed fifteen

The New York Times,
July 13, 1916

SHARK GLIDES UP SHALLOW CREEK, KILLS BOY AND MAN, THEN TEARS ANOTHER SWIMMER IN ESCAPING

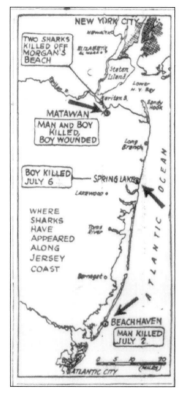

New York Herald,
July 13, 1916

SCENE ON MATAWAN CREEK WHERE SHARK KILLED TWO PERSONS ✚ INDICATES WHERE STILLWELL AND FISHER WERE ATTACKED

in the open Jersey countryside. In a while it began to rain. The rain kept down the dust but slowed him further, and by the time he crossed a small bridge and followed the trolley into Keyport, it was six o'clock. The creature had struck in Matawan a mile and a half upcreek, but to understand what the creature was, John Nichols wanted to see the mouth of the creek where it first came up and where he might catch it leaving. He parked, stepped out of the roadster, and stood in his slicker looking down toward the bay and the creek head.

The death of Lester Stilwell and mauling of Stanley Fisher twenty-two miles south of New York City had drawn the ichthyologist to the tidal creek the following day. If any man could solve the mystery of their attacks, John Nichols believed it was he, and he had vowed to "be present when the ravager was captured."

According to Nichols's desk diaries, he had turned his sights away from the baffling deaths of Charles Bruder the previous week and Vansant the week before that, hoping that the sea had resolved the problem. But the third and fourth attacks in two weeks along the coast had startled Nichols that morning. He had sought out Frederic Lucas, and Dr. Lucas was glad to send his young protégé to Matawan to investigate the matter, for to Dr. Lucas the attacks were evolving from annoyance toward crisis. Moreover, he was confident there was no finer man for the job than John Nichols. Like Lucas, Nichols was convinced the ocean attacks on Vansant and Bruder were not the work of a shark. Now the attacks on Stilwell and Fisher all but confirmed it. Sharks, as far as Nichols knew, did not go up tidal creeks, but his leading suspect was quite happy in a narrow inlet. John Nichols envisioned himself as a detective, and in Matawan Creek he expected to find the fingerprints of *Orcinus orca*, the killer whale.

Yet, as he made his way down to the mouth of Matawan Creek in the rain and authorities introduced him to fishermen in the small port village, the ichthyologist quietly assembled facts that challenged his theory. Surveying the narrow creek at Keyport, Nichols could see plainly that an adult killer whale, thirty feet long and ten thousand pounds, would have trouble navigating the tidal cut, particularly when the tide went out and the creek was a foot deep. Witnesses also undermined his theory—no one had seen something Nichols expected to find, the characteristic spouting of the whale as it moved.

To Nichols's surprise, a number of witnesses described the creature they had seen in the creek in some detail. Unlike the confused and uncertain witnesses at Spring Lake and Beach Haven, all swore it was a shark. Jerry

New York World,
July 13, 1916

Hollohan reported the fish was a big shark that appeared "about ten feet long and weighed probably two hundred and fifty pounds, maybe more." George Burlew's memory of the shark that seized Stanley Fisher was a shark "nine or ten feet long" with a huge tail, almost exactly matching Captain Cottrell's report of the fish he'd seen moving upcreek toward town the day before.

The eyewitnesses excited Nichols's scientific curiosity, although he was careful to temper his enthusiasm around men experiencing the trauma of a tragedy. Nichols presumed all the attacks were the work of a single creature. It defied logic that more than one marine animal was suddenly stalking human beings. For the first time, he seriously considered the possibility that the man-eater was a shark. But the ichthyologist remained doubtful.

At the old Matawan House Hotel, agitated men with guns and drinks in their hands held court with newspapermen and newsreel photographers, and Nichols heard wild talk of sea monsters. Bounty hunters with rifles drifted through the lobby along with fishermen, merchants, and friends and families of the victims. Knowledgeable men insisted the idea that sharks were in the creek "was a myth, pure and simple."

The storm was building to a fury. Black clouds extended up the Jersey coast and across to Long Island. Leaning into the wind, John Nichols hunkered through the darkness and the rain toward the shouts at the creek. No shark had been spotted, but men continued to kill anything that stirred. Dynamite blasts rent the creek, whereupon bubbles appeared that were mistaken for signs of the shark's presence, leading to shouts of "Shark!" and more dynamite. Patiently, Nichols moved among them, explaining that dynamite would never find the man-eater, and as for bullets, "a shark's

FIVE BIG SHARKS TRAPPED IN MATAWAN CREEK AND SCORES AWAIT LOW TIDE TO KILL THEM

MATAWAN CREEK AT LOW TIDE WITH DREDGERS SEEKING STILWELL'S BODY

ARTHUR E. SMITH FIRST TO DIVE FOR STILLWELL.

ALBERT O'HARA STRUCK BY SHARK'S TAIL AS IT SEIZED STILLWELL.

nets as a temporary barrier, which was not broken.

Mayor Walling was joined by Arthur A. Van Buskirk, Recorder of the Borough of Keyport, in the effort to assure the killing or capture of the five sharks. Commodore John Weseman, of the Keyport Yacht Club, who had ordered the bathing houses closed early yesterday, was immediately informed of the presence of the sharks in the creek. He called upon the club members to help, and William Woolley, Jr., and several others immediately got out their motor boats and went to the creek to prevent the escape of the sharks while the barrier at the bridge was being constructed. William Hitchcock, president of the Bayside Gun Club, at Keyport, also co-operated, and members of that club, including Lloyd Armstrong, Palmer Armstrong, Harold Hendrickson and Mr. Hitchcock, got out their heavy weather oilskins and hunting

he was first to dive into the creek in search for Stillwell's body.

Fisher, who was killed, dived just after Smith. Paul R. Dolan, a conductor of the Central of New Jersey Railroad, was with them.

"When Fisher, George Burlew, Smith and myself went down to see about the boys' story of the shark getting Stillwell," said Dolan, "it was an hour and a half after Stillwell had gone. We saw the same boys in swimming and we did not believe the story. Smith said he would dive if he could get tights big enough for him. He and Fisher got tights and I could not get any. Smith dived in first and then Fisher. They were treading water trying for the body when Fisher was caught by the shark.

Mr. J. D. Nichols, of the American Museum of Natural History, went to Matawan yesterday to investigate the shark invasion of these waters. He is

New York Herald, July 14, 1916

thick, tough skin would hardly take an impression from buckshot and would probably turn the .32-caliber bullets fired off them." He also warned that the fish being killed in the creek could attract sharks. But men proceeded as if Nichols were a specter.

Lightning would fell trees around the region that evening and set houses afire and strike and kill two horses and three men working on railroad tracks miles away. But by five-thirty the next morning, the storm had blown over and the sun warmed the tranquil waters of Matawan Creek. The muddy banks dried and the tide came in clean, as if the rage from men and heavens was spent or had never happened. One by one, the dozens of shark hunters had gone home; William Stilwell had at last retired. Edward Craven was walking like a dead man along the creek, his rifle crooked in tired arms, about to turn in himself, when he saw something large moving in the creek. It must have just surfaced, for other shark hunters had recently passed this way and seen nothing.

Craven gripped his rifle and hurried closer, charged with adrenaline. If it was the shark, Ed Craven wanted to blast it out of the water. But the thing in the creek was rocking listlessly with the lap of the tide. If it was a fish, it was a big one and already dead. If it was the shark, the village's worries were over and he would deliver the good news. Scrambling down the muddy bank to get a closer look at the floating mass, he realized with a lurch that the thing was a body.

Wary of touching the body himself, Craven ran to get Constable Mulsoff, who called the Monmouth County coroner. Shortly thereafter, the body was lifted easily onto the dilapidated dock from which Lester Stilwell had dived two days earlier. The small face was badly swollen but smooth and clearly belonged to Stilwell. The face was unmarked, but the rest of the boy was scarcely recognizable. The left side of the abdomen, the left shoulder, and the right breast had been eaten away. The left ankle had been chewed off. The flesh between the hip and the thigh had been mangled, and the stomach had been ripped open as if by giant claws. Authorities carried Lester Stilwell to his home to confirm his identity. Bill Stilwell must have been sleeping after his long nights at the creek, for Luella Stilwell answered the door, and when she saw what the men had brought her, she screamed and collapsed. Burial took place that afternoon after a small service in the Stilwell home.

Numbed by grief, the shark hunters would return to the creek with their boats and guns and hooks, trolling for the man-eater, but on the third day a carnival atmosphere prevailed. Extra-large charges were set to push white geysers dramatically high above the creek for the benefit of the newsreels. It was a fine, clear day for pictures, and with newspaper photographers lining the banks, the shark hunters focused angry gazes at the camera lens instead of at the water. Women posed, grinning, for photographers while angling rifles toward their own toes instead of the creek. The earnest shark hunters seemed a ragged and quixotic bunch to the crowds from miles around that now appeared on the banks, for the shark and the

Matawan shark hunters, 1916

suffering of the small town had become a novelty. "Society turned to shark hunting as the latest wrinkle in summer pastimes," the *Philadelphia Inquirer* reported. "Almost 100 automobiles were packed along the bank of the creek today, and fashionably dressed women and girls from Jersey coast resorts tripped down to the water's edge to watch the shark hunters at work."

That afternoon a newspaperman from New York City rode a motorboat downcreek to the mouth at Raritan Bay and inspected the steel nets erected to contain the shark. Shortly afterward, he reported that Matawan had lost its battle with the sea monster. A large hole had been chewed in the steel nets, and the chunks of meat set as bait were gone.

THE SHARK EMERGENCY

The great white shark moved in the wide curve of the bay between New Jersey and Staten Island. Matawan Creek was miles away. Against considerable odds, the shark had survived battles with men, withstood and escaped the brackish, shallow creek, and sought the freedom of the sea. But this womb of the sea was a hostile place as well—the great white somehow failed to capture the fish that abounded, its normal prey, and it continued on a strange and aberrant course.

As the great white swam in the lower New York bays, it was attracted to other lures. The shark had probably never shared the water with so many boats, large shadows that bewitched it with sonic and scent signals. Sharks are drawn to boats, scientists believe, by electromagnetic impulses emitted by ship equipment, by the metal flashing of propellers, by the skipping of oars across the surface. Sharks crash into boats with exploratory bumps, and they are drawn by bait fish or recently caught fish. There is a contemporary account of an eight-foot blue shark leaping entirely out of the water and landing square on the snoozing form of an astounded young charter fisherman lying on the bottom of a boat, sleeping off seasickness while his friends fished for sharks. The young man awakened, fainted straightaway, and recovered to help his friends beat the shark to death.

Yet of all shark species, the great white is most notorious for attacks on boats. Shark researcher Xavier Maniguet refers mostly to the great white when he writes, "It is clear that a shark heading, even at a slow speed, for the hull of a boat can shatter it like a walnut. No wooden or plastic hull can withstand such a 'snoutbutt.'"

Late in the evening of July 14, a fisherman in the bay returned to shore with a battered boat and an eerie story. He had been cruising along when a big shark attacked his boat and tried to sink it. After a prolonged struggle, the fisherman prevailed in escaping from the shark, but not before he saw it close up: a great dark fish approximately eight feet long.

The great white that had escaped Matawan Creek, the big fish that had attacked five men in unprecedented frenzy, is as likely a suspect in that boat attack as the ocean could produce, yet it cannot be proven. What is known is that on that Friday the moon was nearly full, and the shark was intense with need, and as it cruised Raritan Bay there sounded a rich and confusing cocktail of scents and sonic bursts, boats and mammals.

North and east lay all the bays and harbors and beaches of New York City.

Gertrude Hoffman stepped delicately into the ocean and began to wade out. Thousands of bathers shared the water with Hoffman on the Coney Island and Brighton beaches and all along the Brooklyn shoreline. Wednesday had hit ninety-one degrees, the hottest day of the summer until Thursday, when the mercury "aviated toward ninety-two," the weathermen said. Friday, July 14, was another sizzler, and the Weather Bureau in Washington declared no end in sight to the heat wave.

New Yorkers were escaping to the beach early. The Sea Beach trains and electric streetcars rumbled in all morning from the boroughs, and steamboats from Manhattan disgorged passengers at Coney Island's Dreamland Pier.

Shortly after wading out, Gertrude Hoffman slipped into the waves and began to swim, her slender arms arcing gracefully. She had swum several hundred feet when terror stole her breath. A large, dark fin appeared in the water, moving swiftly directly toward her, and she believed she was about to be devoured by the man-eater of New Jersey.

BIG, SAVAGE SHARKS INFEST COAST IS BELIEF, AS SEARCHERS PURSUE FOUR WHERE MONSTER KILLED TWO

SURVIVORS AND SCENE OF SHARK ATTACK; CREW HUNTING MONSTERS

JOSEPH DUNN.

Sheepshead Bay Swimmer Tells of Attack, Shows Wound — Sea Wolves Chased by Motor Boat and Fired at in Matawan Creek — Mouth of Stream Closed by Nets in Effort at Trapping — 17-Foot Man-Eater Taken at Sea Bright and More Elsewhere.

MATAWAN CREEK Where the TRAGEDIES OCCURRED

ALBERT O'HARA HIT by SHARK

R. GALL and A. F. DAVISON GUNNING for SHARKS

New York World,
July 14, 1916

Fortunately, *The New York Times* reported, Hoffman "had the presence of mind to remember that she had read in the *Times* that a bather can scare away a shark by splashing, and she beat up the water furiously."

The large fin disappeared and Hoffman retreated to shore, where slowly her heart resumed its normal beat. Later, when she regained composure, she wasn't sure if she had seen a shark or merely imagined it after reading the headlines in the morning paper. In any case, she was not eager to return to the water.

While Gertrude Hoffman's encounter in Coney Island was frightening, it was not at all unusual. Reports of sharks nearing the coast were multiplying. A shark panic unrivaled in American history was sweeping along the coasts of New York and New Jersey and spreading by telephone and wireless, letter and postcard. Newsboys chased men down the street:

"Big, savage sharks infest coast!"

"Shark kills 2 bathers, maims 1, near New York!"

"Whole of Jersey coast infested with man-eating monsters!"

"Ten pounds of his flesh ripped off by sea monster!"

The *New York Herald* headline trumpeted six columns across the top, a size reserved for war or the second coming: "Shark Glides Up Shallow Creek and Kills Boy and Man, Then Tears Another Swimmer."

"First Little Victim Only 12 Years Old."

"Man Who Goes to Rescue Dies Soon After Being Dragged from Creature's Teeth."

The morning of Gertrude Hoffman's encounter, Thomas Richard was bathing in Sheepshead Bay when fifty people breakfasting on the porch of a hotel yelled, "Shark!" A group of bathers ran screaming from the water, but Richard was too far out to swim quickly ashore and saw a fin headed in his direction. As the fin closed in, he raced for a nearby motorboat and climbed in, drawing his legs out of the water a fraction of a second before the ripple passed where he had been.

New York Tribune,
July 14, 1916

TIGER SHARKS SEEK PREY OFF CITY BEACHES

Two Bathers, Man and Woman, Pursued at Sheepshead Bay.

MATAWAN CREEK HUNTERS SEE 10

Long Island and Jersey Coasts Seem Infested with Man-Eaters.

Fear rounded the bays of New York. By Saturday, July 15, the weekend business of the bathhouse owners at Coney Island and Brighton Beach was in ruins. Police estimated fifty thousand Coney Island bathers had chosen to stay out of the water for fear of the man-eater. "Terror of Sharks Keeps a Million Bathers on Shore," the *New York World* reported. Crowds frolicking in the water and cooling under umbrellas had been replaced by gangs of men with gaffs and spears, guns and harpoons. "Bathing has come almost to a stop," *The New York Times* reported, "and a new sport, and public service, the hunting of sharks, has sprung up."

Shark Shooting Becomes a Sport
Since Man Eaters Have Become Bold

MR. E. F. WARNER, WITH REVOLVER, AND MR. HERBERT SAVAGE CATCHING A SHARK AT BEACH HAVEN, N. J.

New York Herald,
July 13, 1916

Sportsmen with Harpoons Kill Many Sharks in Chases in Great South Bay

MAN EATING SHARK CAUGHT BY CAPTAIN JOHN R. HOWELL, BAYSHORE L.I.

ALL READY TO HARPOON THE SHARK

THROWING THE HARPOON

THE LOOKOUT

New York Herald,
July 14, 1916

Thus one of the most profligate shark hunts in history swept the coast. Fishermen slew dozens of purported man-eaters and hauled their bloodied corpses to shore, where crowds watched the stomachs of the monsters slit open, revealing immense quantities of fish—but not the prize that paid, human flesh.

The Washington Post crowed: "Sharks Cause Panic. Man-Eaters Seen at Numerous Points Along the Atlantic. New York and New Jersey Shores Guarded by Armed Men." That morning, a Baltimore swimming club made plans to hire a shark patrol for their Sunday race on the Chesapeake, and the Maryland state police schooner *May Brown* confirmed that it had spied "big sea monsters" in Annapolis Harbor.

The shark became an American cause célèbre. Giant, toothy sharks grinned from front-page photographs. Ruthless cartoon sharks stalked human prey on the women's pages, and editorial writers wagged about the death of the myth that sharks were harmless. People signed up for special swimming courses that were supposed to teach bathers how to outwit sharks. Letters to the editor advocated that Washington send the entire United States submarine fleet to destroy the shark. Another suggested the bait of a dummy stuffed with explosives and dressed like Lester Stilwell. According to the *Philadelphia Evening Bulletin,* Hermann Oelrichs's famous bet had at last been settled; there was at last "proof sharks bite."

Shoots Shark from Land, Then Gaffs Man-Eater in the Sound

MRS. FRANK DOANE AND SHARK SHOT BY HER HUSBAND FROM HIS BUNGALOW PORCH, AT SUNNYBROOK, LONG ISLAND

Frank Doane and His Wife Board Launch and Kill 250 Pound Monster After It Had Been Wounded

War on Sharks

Special prize of $30.00 surf-casting outfit for the largest man-eating shark caught at any New Jersey Coast Resort before August 31st.

This offer is an additional prize to our $270.00 contest for fishermen. Send for particulars.

Shark Fishing is Royal Sport

Here's a suggestion for all resorts: Arrange for Shark Fishing Parties, anchor the carcass of a horse or other dead animal off shore where its presence will attract the sharks. The gathering of the sharks around the bait will afford opportunity for exciting and rapid-fire sport for innumerable parties of red-blooded sportsmen.

Tackle for Shark Fishing

Every needed equipment Get the right tackle to insure success.

Shark Hooks, 30c up

All other tackle at attractively low prices.

TWO SEASONABLE SPECIALS

$3.50 Life Guard Suits $2

All-wool, worsted white or navy blue Shirt, flannel Trunks and Web Belt

$4.60 Fishing Outfit for . $2.25

Consisting of 32 Two-piece Sea Rod, amateur Reel, upright with drag holding 260 yards of line Six Hooks, Sinker and 50 yards famous Anglesea Cuttyhunk Line

Same Suits With Cotton Shirt $1.50

New York Tribune,
July 15, 1916

New York Herald,
July 19, 1916

Philadelphia Public Ledger,
July 15, 1916

By the middle of July, thousands of citizens of New Jersey had showered telegrams and letters, editorials and telephone calls on Trenton and Washington, begging the U.S. government and the state of New Jersey for help. Dozens of letters went directly to the White House, imploring President Woodrow Wilson to take steps to rid the coast of the monsters. Hundreds of New Jersey citizens cabled Governor James Fielder with a collective alarm.

The economy of the Jersey Shore was in a crisis. During the second week of July, the grand hotels, cottages, and guest houses from Cape May north to Spring Lake reported an average of 75 percent vacancies. Without summer tourist dollars, many communities would have trouble surviving the winter.

Governor Fielder had called a press conference to make an announcement about the shark emergency. Now, he announced to reporters, the state was facing a crisis for which no one had answers. Reflecting on the deaths of three New Jersey men and a boy, the governor gave his opinion that not one but many sea monsters were attacking the state's coastline at continuing peril to human life, yet there was "no possible action that the state could take that would lessen the evil." The governor had no idea what to do, for veteran fishermen and scientists couldn't settle on what the sea monster or monsters were, let alone offer a plan of action. The governor suggested every coastal town in New Jersey should construct shark nets. At the close of his brief address, Governor Fielder urged "the bathers . . . to be careful" and prayed someone would "come forward" with the knowledge to "drive away the sharks."

President Wilson held a Cabinet meeting to discuss "the shark horror gripping the New Jersey coast." Joseph P. Tumulty, a Jersey City lawyer and the president's trusted adviser, urged Wilson to take bold and decisive action. Earlier that morning, Tumulty had cabled the editor of the *Asbury*

Park Press, promising Wilson would "do anything in his power to . . . rid the Jersey coast of the shark menace."

Yet exactly what the president could do about a rogue shark was another matter entirely. The president turned to Treasury Secretary William Gibbs McAdoo to lead a "war on sharks." Shortly after emerging from the Cabinet meeting, McAdoo called a press conference. McAdoo announced that the U.S. Coast Guard and the Bureau of Fisheries would join forces to "rout the sea terrors." The Coast Guard cutter *Mohawk* would sail immediately to the Jersey coast to destroy any or all killer sharks, avenge four deaths, and save the bathing season.

On Saturday, July 15, the "U.S. war on sharks" was the biggest news in *The Washington Post* and front-page headlines across the world. The Coast Guard "would be ordered to do what it could toward clearing the coast of the dangerous fish." The U.S. lifesaving stations all along the East Coast would be involved, too.

That night the *Mohawk* stood at anchor in New York Harbor, where it would remain. For in the days to come, a shark-extermination program along the 127-mile-long New Jersey coast would be judged "impracticable," and the campaign would be abandoned. The federal government's final suggestion to New Jersey and its bathers was the same as Governor Fielder's: Install wire netting and stay in shallow water. John Cole, director of all government lifesaving stations on the New Jersey coast, had a different opinion. "Where there are no nets, the best way to keep from getting bit is to keep out of the water," he said. "I wouldn't go in."

U. S. WAR ON SHARKS

Wilson and Cabinet Make Plans to Prevent More Tragedies.

COAST GUARDS TURN HUNTERS

Federal Cutters Also Are Ordered to Fish for the Monsters.

Bureau of Fisheries Issues Warning, but Admits Inability to Prevent Attacks—Bacharach Asks Congress for $5,000 to Aid the Campaign. Theories of Scientists for the Presence of Maneaters on the Coast.

The Washington Post,
July 15, 1916

FISHING

The two men were going fishing in the Raritan Bay, hoping to catch lunch or even dinner if the fishing was good. In the early hours of Friday, July 14, the sky was cloudy, but the bay was calm. The men had been lingering on the small wharf in the old port town of South Amboy when Michael Schleisser found an old oar handle lying on the wharf. The oar was snapped in half, the paddle gone, but Schleisser picked it up and put it with his fishing gear.

"What do you need that for?" John Murphy asked his friend.

"Oh, it'll come in handy for something," Schleisser said.

Michael Schleisser was one of the foremost taxidermists in the United States, specializing in turning out impressive trophies for hunters and fishermen. He was renowned as an animal trainer, and he was a big-game hunter who'd traveled the world and stalked the African veldt. In the backyard of his house in Harlem were a tethered black bear, a gray wolf, a red fox, an opossum, and several large alligators in a tank, as well as an aviary, several turtles, a cage of white rats, and other animals. On the second floor were cases displaying mounted rare butterflies, racks of firearms, rows of animal heads, and stuffed animals from Asia, Africa, and South America. Michael Schleisser had trained or killed everything that moved, and was afraid of nothing.

John Murphy knew his way around boats. He worked as a laborer for a steamship company. Together the men loved to fish the bay.

The launch was small, an eight-foot wooden motorboat, but ideal for two men fishing. When Schleisser and Murphy reached Raritan Bay

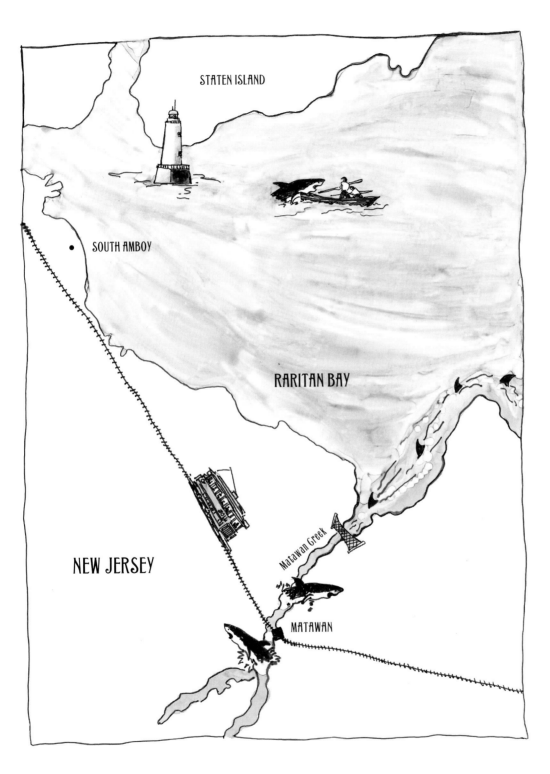

STATEN ISLAND

SOUTH AMBOY

RARITAN BAY

Matawan Creek

NEW JERSEY

MATAWAN

below Staten Island, they threw a six-foot net over the stern and began to trawl the bay with it. The net was great for snagging bait fish like tunny and menhaden. After an hour, they were motoring roughly four miles from the mouth of Matawan Creek.

Shortly before noon, the boat slammed to a halt. Schleisser and Murphy hit the floor, hands out to protect themselves. The force was such that the engine immediately sputtered and died. But the men knew they weren't having engine trouble. As Schleisser and Murphy righted themselves, they saw that something was caught in the net, something big. The boat began to move backward, stern first, against the waves. Water leapt the gunwales. The boat was being pulled backward fast and dragged down. It was being pulled under.

Schleisser, his heart raging, focused his gaze behind the boat. He turned back to Murphy and shouted, "My God, we've got a shark!" The small craft moved backward rapidly. The rushing of the shark threw the bow high in the air and more water rushed over the gunwales. Murphy threw himself forward to keep the stern from being submerged. Schleisser searched the boat for a weapon. There was nothing at hand but their fishing rods and bait and the broken oar handle. Schleisser grabbed it and edged back toward the stern.

To his astonishment, the shark was rising out of the net and onto the stern, snapping its great jaws. Perhaps only a hunter as experienced as Schleisser could consider the creature attacking him without losing all hope. The mouth that Schleisser faced over the gunwales was wide enough to swallow him. As the boat rocked wildly, the shark splashed water vigorously with its powerful tail. The great white was trying to leap the gunwales to reach the two men. As the boat thrashed on the bay, Schleisser tried to steady himself to attempt a blow at the creature's head, but each time he set to swing, "he was thwarted by the rocking of the boat."

Finding his footing for an instant, Schleisser struck with all his strength. The first blow landed on the nose, the second about the gills. The shark responded furiously, rising directly toward Schleisser's arm. The great jaws missed their target, but the immense head struck Schleisser's forearm hard, its sandpaper-like skin opening cuts on Schleisser's wrist. The shark thrashed wildly, entangling itself further in the mesh of the net. With a desperate rush it leapt onto the stern toward the men. Schleisser saw an opportunity and struck another heavy blow on the nose, which partially stunned the shark. As it lay dazed for a moment on the stern, Schleisser struck it again and again on the gills and the head until the fish went slack and slowly slid into the net. Schleisser and Murphy fell back into the boat exhausted, near collapse. The shark was dead. They had beaten it to death.

Stunned, the men sat silently, unable to move or talk as the boat gently rocked on the bay. Moving slowly, they got the engine to turn over and chugged back toward Amboy, towing the dead shark.

Michael Schleisser and John Murphy clambered onto the docks with the ragged look of men who had nothing left to give. Wearily, Schleisser described the battle with the shark. The big-game hunter admitted the shark had attacked more ferociously than any African lion or any grizzly bear he had ever encountered. It was, he said, "the hardest fight for life I've ever had."

Eagerly, men on the wharf helped Schleisser and Murphy hoist the giant fish from its tow. It took half a dozen men to carry it. Michael Schleisser announced that he wanted a picture, and hastily the massive shark was propped on a pair of sawhorses some seven feet apart. The taxidermist stood unsmiling behind his trophy, his torso nearly obscured by the height of the dorsal fin. The fish's dark, unseeing eyes stared out in a kind of fury, and its jaw was propped open wide enough to take in a man's head.

In the following days, while Michael Schleisser investigated the true nature of his trophy, John Nichols and Robert Murphy resolved to undertake their own search for the shark. On Wednesday, July 20, the scientists set out in their small launch into Jamaica Bay, which they had determined was a likely destination for a hungry shark that had demonstrated a northward progression of attacks—if it had not yet escaped to the sea. Murphy stood in the bowsprit of the small craft, a harpoon in one hand. At the wheel, John Nichols piloted the vessel and scanned the waters for a caudal fin on the surface—for Nichols and Murphy now had no doubt that it was a great white they were hunting.

Like Frederic Lucas, neither Murphy nor Nichols had been inclined to believe any shark was a deliberate man-eater, but the past thirty-six hours had altered their view. In Matawan four days earlier, Nichols had been influenced by his meeting with Captain Watson Fisher, Stanley Fisher's father. Captain Fisher claimed that, in his fifty-six years at sea, he had never seen a shark attack a man and never knew of an authentic report of such an attack. Yet Fisher emphasized to Nichols his new-found conviction that his son was killed by a shark.

Retreating to the depths of the American Museum of Natural History in New York, Nichols had pored over rafts of old documents. His research led him to believe that not only was Frederic Lucas wrong, but scientific and government assurances about the harmlessness of sharks were both uninformed and dangerous. New Jersey was correct to have "abandoned its swimming," he had told *The New York Times*, and now it was "time for New Yorkers to take warning. It is the white shark which has been at work, and my own belief is that [this] single fish . . . has killed all four of the bathers and that if . . . it is killed the attacks will end."

Subsequently, in a humbling if not devastating moment, Dr. Lucas admitted on the front page of *The New York Times* that he had been wrong. With the headline "Science Admits Its Error. No Longer Doubted That Big Fish Attack Men," the *Times* reported that "the foremost authority on sharks in this country has doubted that any type of shark ever attacked a human being, but the recent cases have changed his view."

So Nichols and Murphy set out into the waters of Jamaica Bay to fish for the big shark. They had armed themselves with several harpoons. Guns and knives were also aboard, to the extent they would matter. The scientists were under no illusions about their chances versus *Carcharodon carcharias* if it appeared in its full-grown size. They cruised the deep channel in Rockaway Inlet. Nichols could see some distance through the water, paying special attention to sandbars, against which the sun would silhouette his quarry. The white shark rode high in the water, announcing its presence like a surfacing U-boat.

Suddenly Nichols felt his heart protesting against his ribs. He had spotted a shark. Nichols carefully worked the sloop toward it, following the winding course of the shark. Murphy finally saw an elusive shadow moving a couple of boat lengths ahead. The light in the water could play tricks with the shadow, blowing it up to monstrous size, but then the shadow slipped too far ahead to discern its true substance. Murphy tightened his grip on the harpoon.

As the huge shadow darted, Murphy readied himself for the possibility it might turn and shoot under the bowsprit, giving him but a fraction of an instant to strike. He knew well the consequence of a bad throw—he'd watch the iron graze the fish and "the pole stand quivering in the sand, while the shark darts away into deep water and is gone." He

The New York Times,
July 14, 1916

was not sure anymore if he knew the consequence of a good throw. What was a harpoon to an enraged three-thousand-pound fish: a bothersome needle? Should he pray it would come close enough for the guns and the knives? Or pray that it wouldn't?

When the shark came within striking distance, Murphy surged forward, heart drumming, hoisting the harpoon, angling for purchase on the bowsprit. But the fearsome shadow was what Nichols and Murphy immediately recognized as a sand shark, a common, large, fish-eating species. With dismay the men exhaled, perhaps for a moment doubting their pursuit of a white shark.

The shark disappeared and the scientists spent the day and the night looking for larger shadows in the bay. Other sharks appeared, but nothing to arouse their interest. Nichols and Murphy discussed leaving Jamaica Bay and guarded against the unwelcome feeling that the trip was turning into a failure.

As the sun came up on the second day, Nichols and Murphy trailed steel hooks on strong chains baited with the "tempting morsel" of a cow's lung. Animal blood radiated and diffused in the water as the launch rode the gentle bay, bearing the long shadows of men on the waters they had known since boyhood, which now seemed somehow alien.

Philadelphia Press, July 10, 1916

THE SHARK WOULD ENDURE

There was nothing left to do but cut open the fish to see what its stomach contents revealed, but Michael Schleisser disappointed his audience. Instead he recruited men to lift the huge creature into his automobile.

Back at home, Schleisser worked quickly, for the fish would decay rapidly. That afternoon, in the basement given over to a taxidermy studio, Schleisser began the enormous task of mounting the shark. It measured seven and a half feet long and weighed 350 pounds. It was a dark, dull blue on top and white underneath. Schleisser cut the fish open and removed the stomach, whereupon a terrible odor filled the basement, and the taxidermist found himself sorting through a large, grisly pile of flesh and bones. There was a mix of large and small bones, and the bones appeared to be human. Schleisser weighed the flesh and bones together and they came to approximately fifteen pounds.

As he studied the gruesome scene in the dim light of his basement, Schleisser came to believe he had caught the man-eating shark that had terrorized New Jersey. As Schleisser began to mount the shark, that Tuesday, July 14, President Wilson had already suspended the war on sharks, and John Nichols and Robert Murphy were making plans to hunt the predator in Jamaica Bay, unaware that an apparent man-eater had been caught. Schleisser, a showman at heart, felt no immediate need to inform the world. He wanted to confirm that the bones in the shark's stomach were human, and for that he required the assistance of a scientist. Schleisser resolved to ship the bones to the most famous scientist he personally knew, one whose word was beyond reproach. But first he made a phone call to his local newspaper.

The newspaper was in a hurry to get the story out, but recognizing the publicity value of having the shark to display, the editors were willing to hold the story until Schleisser had completed his taxidermy. Four days later, Schleisser brought the stuffed and mounted shark to the offices of the newspaper. The next day, the *Home News* proudly devoted its front page to one of the most dramatic stories in its history, with the headline: "Harlem Man in Tiny Boat Kills a 7$_{1/2}$ Foot Man-Eating Shark."

Bronx Home News,
July 19, 1916

Harlem Man In Tiny Boat Kills A 7½ Foot Man-Eating Shark

Beats It to Death With Broken Oar, Directly Off Matawan Creek, Where Two Bathers Were Attacked and Killed By Sea-Tiger Last Week—Examination By Director of Museum of Natural History Shows Human Bones in Shark's Stomach.

The 7½ ft. Man-Eater and the Man Who Killed It.

The Shark can be seen in The Home News Window to-day and to-morrow until 10.30 p. m.

That day and the next, Thursday, July 20, the newspaper promised its readers "the monster will be placed in the window of the *Home News,* at 135 W. 125th St., where everyone will have an opportunity to see what a man-eating shark really looks like." Next to the man-eater, the *Home News* promised, would be a display of the large and small bones found in its stomach.

The box had arrived in the middle of the week at the American Museum of Natural History, addressed to the director, Frederic Lucas. It was not unusual for the museum to receive a box of dry bones, poison adders, or shrunken heads, for that matter. This box received special attention because an accompanying note claimed that the bones the box contained had been retrieved from the stomach of the man-eating shark.

Lucas would have treated the claim with his usual skepticism had it not come from someone he knew and trusted. And before him, unquestionably, was a pile of masticated human bones. Although the bones challenged his theory, Dr. Lucas was grateful to Schleisser and wrote a note on museum stationery thanking the taxidermist.

> Dear Mr. Schleisser: I am very much obliged to you for your courtesy in letting me see the bones taken from the shark. They are parts of the left radius and ulna of one of the anterior left ribs. There is no doubt about this. They have, as you see, been badly shattered. Can you tell me the exact species of shark from which these bones were taken, or if you are in doubt, I am sure that Mr. Nichols would be very glad to call and determine the species exactly? Again thanking you for your kindness, I am, F.A. LUCAS, Director.

From Brooklyn and Staten Island and Greenwich Village they came. Thousands clambered aboard the trolleys to 125th Street in Harlem. By the time John Nichols arrived at the *Home News* office, a mob of thirty thousand people had gathered. Nichols pushed to the front and lingered, staring at the man-eater. His first glance eliminated all doubt. It was unquestionably *Carcharodon carcharias*.

Independent experts had determined that the bones taken from the shark's stomach were human. Physicians identified the eleven-inch bone as the shinbone of a boy—presumably Lester Stilwell's—and a section of rib bone as belonging to a young man, perhaps Charles Bruder. Dr. Lucas, however, maintained these judgments were "incorrect." The bones were certainly human, Lucas agreed, but they were parts of the left forearm and left upper rib taken from the body of a robust man who had been "dead some time and not the result of any active attack." This was not proof, in Dr. Lucas's opinion, that a shark could bite clean through human bone, or that sharks attack man. This conclusion supported Dr. Lucas's lifework as well as his theory that the species of the attacker was unknown. In a letter to Bureau of Fisheries Commissioner Hugh Smith, Lucas declared that the great white with human remains inside was not the killer.

On August 8, 1916, Hugh Smith wrote Frederic Lucas: "The excitement in this matter appears to have died down, much to the relief of this office, and I hope nothing will occur to resuscitate it."

By the end of that summer of 1916, the last summer before America entered the Great War, the great white shark had fallen from the front pages. But the shark would endure in the American imagination.

On July 10, 1917, in the one-year anniversary week of the attacks, five hundred bathers fled screaming from the waters of Rockaway Park after swimmers spied a large fin near shore. Over the next few decades, New York newspapers sounded what became an annual alarm, and the parents of Matawan forbade their children from swimming in Matawan Creek.

And still the great white lives, in the depths where it has always reigned: in cautionary tales told by mothers and fathers, in whispers in the unconscious, in offshore shadows, and in ripples on a tidal creek.

EPILOGUE

Today all evidence of the great white shark of that long-ago summer is gone. The carcass of the fish disappeared shortly after it was displayed in the window of the *Home News*, and some years later, a scientist spotted its jaw hanging in a window of a Manhattan shop before it disappeared forever. Yet it was the legacy of this young, aberrant, perhaps sickly or injured great white to frame the way people perceive sharks. In 1974, Peter Benchley invoked the 1916 shark as the role model for his fictional white shark in *Jaws*.

By the end of the twentieth century, the deadly predator of 1916 immortalized by Benchley would begin to fade from popular culture. By the 1990s, the concept of the rogue shark had fallen out of scientific favor for lack of proof other than anecdotal material.

Indeed, by the twenty-first century, *Carcharodon carcharias* had assumed a new status as a magnificent yet misunderstood sea creature, a rare and accidental killer of man, an endangered species protected by the laws of numerous countries, including the United States. So radical was the change in attitude that in 2000 Peter Benchley pleaded with Australians not to destroy a great white that had killed a young swimmer. "This was not a rogue shark, tantalized by the taste of human flesh and bound now to kill and kill again. Such creatures do not exist, despite what you might have derived from *Jaws*. . . . Let us mourn the man and forgive the animal, for, in truth, it knew not what it did."

Hermann Oelrichs, whose 1891 reward was never collected, would have appreciated Benchley's view.

SOURCES AND ACKNOWLEDGMENTS

This is a work of nonfiction. All characters are real, and their descriptions, actions, and dialogue are based on dozens of interviews; hundreds of contemporary newspaper accounts; turn-of-the-century diaries and letters, medical and scientific journals, birth and death records, census records, theses, films, and academic transcripts; research in more than twenty museums and libraries; and information from several hundred books on sharks, the oceans, tides, the history of science and medicine, man-eating animals, shipwrecks and sea monsters, Victorian love poems, Philadelphia, the Jersey Shore, novels and plays of the era, and every aspect of American history and culture that I imagined would have affected the lives of people in 1916.

To reconstruct the life of a shark in 1916 presented unique challenges, and this would have been a book-out-of-water without George Burgess, ichthyologist, shark biologist, and Coordinator of Museum Operations of the Florida Museum of Natural History at the University of Florida in Gainesville. As director of the International Shark Attack File (ISAF), George studies contemporary and historic shark attacks as closely as anyone in the world. Anyone seeking information about shark attacks should look at the ISAF Web site, www.flmnh.ufl.edu/fish/Sharks/sharks.htm.

With George Burgess, I rode a boat up Matawan Creek, reconstructing the path of the shark, and attempted to fix the location of the steamboat dock attacks by global positioning system. George Burgess and I examined the sites of all four shark fatalities of 1916; his on-site estimate of the salinity of Matawan Creek was part of the evidence that led him, and me, to believe a great white shark could have passed up the creek. The National Oceanographic and Atmospheric Administration provided computer projections of the tide in Matawan Creek in July 1916.

The following is only a small sampling of the books I consulted for *Close to Shore*, but these stand out as the most helpful, so I offer them as a guide for those wishing to pursue the topics discussed in this book.

Able, Kenneth W., and Michael Fahay. *The First Year in the Life of Estuarine Fishes in the Middle Atlantic Bight*. New Brunswick, NJ: Rutgers University Press, 1998.

Allen, Frederick Lewis. *Only Yesterday: An Informal History of the 1920's*. 1931. New York: HarperPerennial, 2000.

Baldridge, H. David. *Shark Attack*. New York: Berkley, 1978.

Bosker, Gideon, and Lena Lencek. *The Beach: The History of Paradise on Earth*. New York: Viking, 1998.

Burt, Nathaniel. *The Perennial Philadelphians: The Anatomy of an American Aristocracy.* Boston: Little, Brown, 1963.

Churchill, Allen. *Remember When: A Loving Look at Days Gone By: 1900–1942.* New York: Golden Press, 1967.

Coppleson, V. M. *Shark Attack.* Sydney, Australia: Agnus and Robertson, 1958.

Ellis, Richard, and John E. McCosker. *Great White Shark: The Definitive Look at the Most Terrifying Creature of the Ocean.* New York: HarperCollins Publishers in collaboration with Stanford University Press, 1991.

Fernicola, Richard G. *In Search of the Jersey Man-Eater.* Deal, NJ: George Marine Library, 1987.

Fox, Dixon Ryan, and Arthur M. Schlesinger Sr., editors. *A History of American Life.* The 1948 thirteen-volume set abridged and revised by Mark C. Carnes. New York: Scribner, 1996.

Gilbert, Perry W., editor. *Sharks and Survival.* Includes "Treatment of Shark-Attack Victims in South Africa" by George D. Campbell and David H. Davies. 1963. Lexington, MA: D.C. Heath & Co., 1975.

Henderson, Helen. *Around Matawan and Aberdeen.* Dover, NH: Arcadia Publishing, 1996.

Himmelfarb, Gertrude. *Victorian Minds: A Study of Intellectuals in Crisis and Ideologies in Transition.* 1952. Chicago: Elephant Paperbacks, 1968.

Klimley, A. Peter, and David G. Ainley, editors. *Great White Sharks: The Biology of Carcharodon carcharias.* San Diego: Academic Press, 1996.

Lloyd, John Bailey. *Eighteen Miles of History on Long Beach Island.* Harvey Cedars, NJ: Down the Shore Publishing and The SandPaper Inc., 1994.

Lloyd, John Bailey. *Six Miles at Sea: A Pictorial History of Long Beach Island.* Harvey Cedars, NJ: Down the Shore Publishing and The SandPaper Inc., 1990.

Lucas, Frederic A. *Fifty Years of Museum Work: Autobiography, Unpublished Papers, and Bibliography.* New York: American Museum of Natural History, 1933.

Murphy, Robert Cushman. *Fish-Shape Paumanok: Nature and Man on Long Island.* Philadelphia: The American Philosophical Society, 1964.

Murphy, Robert Cushman. *Logbook for Grace: Whaling Brig Daisy, 1912–1913.* Alexandria, VA: Time-Life Books, 1982.

Schlereth, Thomas J. *Victorian America: Transformations in Everyday Life, 1876–1915.* 1991. New York: HarperPerennial, 1992.

Wallace, Joseph. *A Gathering of Wonders: Behind the Scenes at the American Museum of Natural History.* New York: St. Martin's Press, 2000.

PHOTO CREDITS

Grateful acknowledgment is made to the following for granting permission to reproduce the photographs and newspaper articles in this book:

The American Museum of Natural History, Department of Library Services: 61, 70. *Bronx Home News*: 134. Brown Brothers Stock Photos: 115. Helen Henderson: 89. John Bailey Lloyd: 20, 21, 22, 23, 24, 25. The Matawan Historical Society: 99. *New York Herald*: 28, 40, 58, 79, 110, 113, 121, 122, 123. *The New York Times*: 6, 28, 109, 131; all articles are copyright © 1916 by the New York Times Co. *New York Tribune*: 108, 120, 123. *New York World*: ii, 66, 112, 119. *Philadelphia Press*: 18, 44, 63, 68, 132. *Philadelphia Public Ledger*: 11, 19, 59, 60, 78, 105, 106, 107, 124. The Spring Lake Historical Society: 43, 50, 52. *The Washington Post*: 81, 125; photos © 1916 *The Washington Post*. James Watt: 73, 86; photos copyright © 2002 James Watt/www.norbertwu.com. Norbert Wu: 13, 48; photos copyright © 2002 Norbert Wu/www.norbertwu.com.

1/28/05
1/05
9/08